CHARLIE
a love story

CHARLIE
a love story

BARBARA LAMPERT

Langdon Street Press

Langdon Street Press
212 3ʳᵈ Avenue North, Suite 290
Minneapolis, MN 55401
612.455.2293
www.langdonstreetpress.com

ISBN: 978-1-936782-25-3
LCCN: 2011940916

Distributed by Itasca Books

Printed in the United States of America

For Charlie, and every other wonderful dog

Foreword

Charlie is one of those rare dogs who leave a lasting impression. Although many people loved him, no one knew him the way Barbara did. Their relationship was extraordinarily close.

I first met Charlie when he was a little more than a year old. Barbara and her husband David had brought him to my veterinary clinic, and when I walked in to see them, Charlie was sitting in Barbara's lap, even though he weighed well over one hundred pounds. When he saw me, he immediately extended his paw in greeting. As large and imposing as Charlie was, his behavior spoke of his kindness and gentleness as well as his loyalty. I will never forget that image, and I think it says a lot about Charlie's character.

Charlie had come in that day because an unusual injury had made it hard for him to use one of his rear legs. Because he was pain-free and otherwise happy, I struggled with making the recommendation to cut through his tibia to straighten his leg. Doing that would restore his mobility and prevent crippling arthritis later in life but would be very painful to endure and also require a lengthy recuperation. But Charlie did have that operation, and he made a great recovery. And for all of us, that was the start of our trusting medical relationship, which has evolved into an enduring friendship.

Charlie was unusually courageous and strong-willed. Throughout his life, and particularly when he got older, he faced his health problems with a determination to overcome them and an acceptance of whatever surgeries and medical regimens he had to endure in the process. Through all those procedures, he continued to hold up his paw in friendship, happily seeing me as his friend, and never once did he hold a grudge. I think Charlie really understood that all of us were working together to give him the best possible quality of life. I could sense that Charlie's focus was to quickly heal and return home to Barbara.

In this very heartfelt, special book, Barbara captures Charlie's character and their relationship with clarity and immediacy. This is a tender yet very real story of the love and devotion of a dog and his master equally beloved of each other, a story I think will always be remembered.

Robert Olds, DVM, Diplomate ACVS
Chief of Surgery, VCA Brentwood Animal Hospital
(formerly Brentwood Pet Clinic)
West Los Angeles, California

Prologue

I love dogs. More than that, I love Golden Retrievers. More than that, I love Charlie.

Charlie's my dog. It's been that way since the beginning. I don't really know how that got started. I just know that as the years have gone on, Charlie and I have become more and more attached. He listens to me, follows me around. No matter how close we are, he tries to figure out how we can be even closer.

In fact, Charlie thinks we're married. I always tell him there are three reasons we can't be: different species, too many years between us, and I'm already married. I don't think any of this matters to Charlie.

Charlie's a big dog, not just physically but in every way. He has a big heart, a big smile, lots of courage, a big appetite, and a great, big, generous spirit. Charlie's the emotional core of our family, the most solid being I have ever known, and wise beyond his years.

Charlie and me. It's a great love affair, a once-in-a-lifetime connection.

Charlie, you make me so happy. When I think of you I smile. Bless you, my big guy. I love you with all my heart and soul.

Let me tell you more about Charlie and me:
Our story takes place in Malibu, California.
It's from a journal I was keeping about my garden,
but as Charlie began to have some health problems,
the journal quickly became mostly about him.

It's June 2001.
Charlie is eleven years old ...

2001

Charlie and me

One

June 13, 2001

I brought my Charlie outside a few times today, so he could be with me while I gardened. I was pruning the lower branches of a eucalyptus, deep in under the tree, and there was Charlie, about two inches away, chewing on the twigs I had cut. That makes him happy. I love seeing that.

I hope we can find some way to either retard or reverse what's going on in his back. It seems stiff, and he's having trouble walking. I will do whatever it takes to care for him. Charlie deserves that, and more. And I'll have him in the garden with me as much as possible, because I know how good that is for him. For me too.

June 17, 2001

The Cecile Brunner roses just finished their first bloom of the year, not one little rose left. I think it's going on three years since I planted them. It's so beautiful when those three now large bushes are in bloom, hundreds of little soft pink roses. And in the early morning and at night their scent is so fragrant. But as quickly as the blooms come up, that's as quickly as they go. Poof.

Since I was very young I have understood how fleeting life is. Now, according to our veterinarian, Dr. Robert Olds, my Charlie, soon to be twelve years old, may have some serious problems with a disk and a nerve in his back.

Charlie had so many things wrong when he was young that I thought I'd be lucky to get eight years with him. At a year and a half, he injured a growth plate in his leg that required major surgery. Over the next few years, he had frequent seizures. When he was four, he scratched his cornea on a tree branch. He has a thyroid problem that makes him overweight and requires medication. Even with the thyroid medication, he still has weighed about one hundred pounds for much of his life, and I know really big dogs don't usually live that long.

But now eleven years is not long enough. So I'll appreciate when the Cecile Brunners bloom again, and I'll continue to give my Charlie lots of love, and be grateful for every minute I can be with him.

June 19, 2001

I love it when Charlie is out in the garden with me. Sometimes I'll be very busy, and I'll look up, and he's just standing there, watching me. I'll call his name or say "Puppy," which is the other name I've used for him his whole life, and he'll gently wag his tail and come ambling over, so relieved that I've stopped to notice him. Of course, I give him as much love as I possibly can, not only because I love him tremendously but also because I know how much it comforts and calms him. I can feel him relax. My Puppy. Seems like yesterday he really was just a puppy. I remember when I first saw him …

It was a Sunday in November, 1989. David and I had walked into Pet Headquarters in Malibu, where I would go pretty regularly to get my "puppy fix," when I spotted what looked like a Golden Retriever, but not quite. He was whitish-blond, with a square, serious face, and big, really big, too big for the small quarters he was in, I thought. So I asked if I could see him.

My only intention was to get him out of his cage and give him a little exercise. I had no thought of getting another dog. We already had Mandy, our first Golden Retriever, who was two years old at the time, and Arthur, our Afghan Hound, who was one and a half. They were just coming out of their puppyhoods, and the house was starting to settle down. I was getting ready to study for my Marriage and Family Therapist licensing exams. I didn't need any more distractions.

First thing the dog did after he was brought out was climb on top of the guinea pig cage. After I got him away, he started running around the store. He looked wild. Some kids began playing with him. Finally I got him to sit with me on the floor, and the kids came over. They wanted to know if I was going to get this dog.

"No," I said, "we already have two dogs, and we already have a Golden Retriever."

I noticed how soft and beautiful his coat was and that, although he was playful, he did not seem very happy. And I wondered how such a big dog had suddenly appeared in the pet store. I'd been there almost every day for weeks. Did someone return him?

I began asking the shopkeeper questions. Where was the dog from? "Missouri." Puppy mill, I thought. How old was he? "Thirteen weeks." So big for thirteen weeks, I thought, and why hasn't he sold? Retrievers sell in a minute in this pet store — they're such great beach and water dogs. Then, for some reason, I asked when the dog was born, and the shopkeeper answered, "August 12th."

No! I couldn't believe it. That's my birthday. David and I looked at each other in disbelief. Can't get another dog, don't want another dog now. I told the shopkeeper that August 12th was my birthday. He gave me an interesting smile and said something like, "Guess it was meant to be."

So David and I played with the dog some more. My mind was spinning. We'd been there for about three hours. Finally we decided we had to go, so the dog went back into his display cage. It was hard to leave him, but we did.

We drove a little, stopped the car, and talked. I'd already thought of a name for him — Charles, because although he was so wild, he looked noble. But amazingly, we went home. We didn't want to make a spur-of-the-moment decision. What about my licensing exams? What about the Golden we already had? What about the fact that we already had two dogs? What about getting a dog in a pet store? And on and on and on.

David said it was up to me, because of my exams and because of the dog's birthday. I couldn't get Charles out of my mind. I started thinking, again, that maybe someone had returned him, that maybe no one would take him because he was thirteen weeks old, did not look purebred, and was so big. Would I always wonder about that dog who was born on my birthday? Would I regret that I did not get him? And I remembered that after I had played with him for a few hours, he seemed happier. In the midst of all this deliberating, somehow his name became Charlie. That felt right.

So Friday morning I called the pet shop. Yes, thankfully, he was still there. Yes, we could put a deposit on him. Yes, we could pick him up that night. The agonizing was over. Charlie was coming home.

Charlie at thirteen weeks, in the kitchen

But he arrived with quite a few insecurities. True, he was housebroken right away, but it took an act of Congress to get him to go out. Every time he'd get to the threshold of the sliding glass door that led outside, he'd stop. For months, David had to carry him out. Charlie just wanted to stay in the house.

Except one day, after he had been with us for some months, and after he had gotten over his fear of going outside, he dug his way out from under the chain-link fence on the far western side of our property. I'm sure he loved what a great hole he'd dug, but in doing that he'd put himself at risk. He was near an open field, just a hop-skip-and-a-jump from the Pacific Coast Highway and any number of other dangerous places.

My heart jumped when I found him there. Mandy and Arthur were on the inside of the fence, and Charlie was on the outside. To get to him, I would have to go all the way across our property, almost an acre, then through the house, out the front door, and then back around just about the entire fence. And I'd have to count on his staying there, even though he was an energetic puppy and didn't look very happy where he was.

So, in my most authoritative voice, I told them all to stay. It seemed like it took forever to get to him. When I finally did, the three of them were sitting in exactly the same positions I had left them in, just staring at each other. I was so relieved. It was such a beautiful sight. I carried Charlie all the way home.

The next day, we bought railroad ties and placed them along the full length of the back fence. He would never be able to get out again. Though he never showed any interest in doing that again, either …

Charlie at fourteen weeks, near the back of our property

Two

June 21, 2001

First official day of summer, and really hot. I kicked it off by spending oh I'd say about ten hours in the garden. My gardener Jésus was with me for six of them. We both worked nonstop, despite the heat.

I've been so worried about Charlie's back and the trouble he's been having walking. Gardening is the only activity that somewhat relieves my mind about him. At one point though, while gardening and listening on our outdoor speakers to a beautiful Van Morrison song — with the words "You fill my heart with gladness, take away my sadness, ease my troubles, that's what you do" — I started crying, because Charlie does all that for me.

My Charlie, my ever-so-loyal companion. More than any other being, he has healed so much of the loneliness I have carried with me since childhood. When I was young, I felt ignored by my parents, who were scarcely interested in what I did in school or with friends. But where I am and what I'm doing matter to Charlie. And when I'm sick or upset he's right by my side, either in bed with me or on the floor by my chair. When I was studying to become a psychotherapist, he often sat with me, even though he was just a puppy.

Yesterday, at another clinic where we'd gone for a second opinion about his back, the staff fell in love with him. While David and I waited with Charlie in the reception area, a technician came out from the back, looked at Charlie, came over, petted him, smiled, and then gave him a kiss on the forehead. Then Charlie got really focused on four kittens in a big cage — he wouldn't take his eyes off them. The receptionist just kept saying, with a big smile on her face, "That's too cute — I wish I had a camera." Now Charlie weighs almost one hundred pounds. He's a big guy, with a big head, and these kittens were as small as teacups.

The doctor smiled too, the whole time she was examining him. Of course, Charlie was doing his thing, where I sit on the floor and he backs up into my lap, like a truck, and then sits.

All his life, people have fallen in love with him. And Charlie has always had a great interest in them. He watches, listens, and often imitates. For instance, David and I kiss when we first see each other. So when either of us walks into the house, Charlie demands to be kissed — and on the lips too. Can't get by him unless we do that. People sleep on pillows, right? Well, when Charlie gets up on our bed, he makes sure his head is on a pillow. And then instantly pretends to be asleep, before someone can tell him to move. His ways are so funny. Our housekeeper calls him "Funny Charlie."

So today I gardened like a maniac, trying to make my worries about Charlie go away. I had him out with me for a while, until I noticed that trying to run was causing him pain in his right leg, then in he went.

June 22, 2001

Just a little watering this morning. I moved a large, beautiful potted bamboo that I have been nursing for a year to a prominent place in the middle of the garden, next to a green wood bench. When I got this bamboo, I was told it needed mostly shade and not much water, but that's totally not the case. Like most potted bamboos, it needs part sun, part shade, and lots of water. Of course, when I did as I'd been advised, it quickly deteriorated. After about two months, it had lost almost all its growth and was mostly brown. It looked horrible. So I put it in a far corner of the garden and watered it often, not really expecting it to recover. But bit by bit, it came back. Now it's full, overflowing its pot, and gorgeous.

When David and I got home from dinner, Charlie was even worse than he'd been, dragging his right foot and limping. I panicked. Off to the emergency hospital. A cortisone shot, a B-12 shot, and a knowledgeable doctor. Now I'm hoping that with rest and the right supplements, the inflammation in his back will subside.

CHARLIE

July 2, 2001

Mostly watering this morning. It's so hot. I keep thinking I could ask Jésus to do it, but then I remember how watering keeps me in touch with every plant and tree.

But I'm torn between doing that and wanting to spend as much time as possible with Charlie, who is struggling right now. So I watered for a bit and then sat with Charlie, trying to get him to lie on his back, to give it a rest. Oh how I miss my Puppy in the garden with me, chewing twigs, coming over wagging his tail, and exploring.

I remember one time when I was outside in the garden, oh maybe five or six years ago …

I looked up from what I was doing and saw Charlie standing over something, wagging his tail and not moving. I called him, but he would not move, which was really unusual. I walked over to him, and as I got closer, he wagged his tail even faster. When I got to him, I still couldn't see anything, so I followed his eyes: Right under his nose was the tiniest bird I had ever seen; it was the size of a thimble. I grabbed Charlie's collar and quickly marched him inside, not realizing at the time that if he had wanted to hurt the bird, he'd already had ample opportunity. At first, I could not figure out what to do. I commended Charlie for pointing the bird out and being so good. Then I called Malibu Wildlife Rescue.

They were out in twenty minutes — three young women, all dressed in khaki Bermuda shorts. I took them to the area where the bird was. But instead of taking the baby bird away, as I had expected they would do, they looked for a nest above — and they found one. Then one of the women stood on the shoulders of another, with the little bird in her gloved hand, and put it back in its nest. I was thrilled, they were happy, and I'm sure that when it recovered its senses, the bird was no longer as scared. What could that little bird have felt, with a one-hundred-plus-pound dog standing over it?

They asked me how I discovered this tiny bird. I told them that Charlie, my Golden Retriever, had discovered it. I told them the story, and then I introduced them to Charlie. He was standing right by the door with what looked like a smile on his face. Seemed really proud of himself. The three young women were incredulous that Charlie had found the bird and had not tried to harm it. "That big Golden?" one of them asked. They left the house shaking their heads. I was so proud of Charlie. He saved that little bird ...

My Charlie, what a kind, gentle soul he is.

Charlie at six years old

Three

July 5, 2001

At about six this morning I was out in the garden watering the back area pretty thoroughly in anticipation of not having much time over the next couple of days. It seems my Charlie is going to have surgery to remove a testicle that has a lump in it. The lump is producing estrogen and causing him to be anemic. And the estrogen may be contributing to the problems in his back.

Later in the morning I took Charlie for pre-surgery blood work at the Brentwood Pet Clinic, Dr. Olds' office. In the waiting room, a woman sitting across from us kept staring at him. Finally, she spoke. "What a sweet dog, and what a sweet face he has." I smiled. Yes he is, and yes he does have. My big Golden.

So in walked a four-month-old Golden Retriever puppy. Fluffy, cute as could be, and playful, of course. She and Charlie sniffed each other face-to-face. The contrast was so apparent — the young and the old. When you first get them, you never think they're going to get older. They always seem like puppies, so young and innocent. But there it was this morning, Charlie's opposite. Not just that Charlie is older, losing hair, and has a bandaged foot and back problems. But there was that little Retriever puppy who could not stop moving, and there was Charlie, standing solid as a rock, and so wise.

July 6, 2001

Charlie had his surgery to remove the one testicle today. Surgery went fine, thank God.

July 13, 2001

Just one of those horrible days. Nothing could make me happy. One week after his surgery, and my Charlie is not doing well. He will be twelve in a month, he's big, and I know he can't last forever. Now he's having trouble keeping anything down. Second-guessing — is it the Baytril antibiotic, the partial neutering, the stupid Chinese herb, a faulty adrenal gland, too much estrogen, basic old age, or something else?

I'm sitting on the sofa while I write this. Charlie is glued to me, his head touching my leg, his paw in my lap. He sits up periodically and raises his paw, but I don't know what he wants. I can only guess: he's hungry. Hasn't had much to eat in the last few days. I can see he's losing weight. But not his spirit — his spirit and heart are big. The veterinarians say we're lucky he's made it to twelve. Dr. Karen Martin, a vet he saw recently, says we're on "bonus time."

None of this makes sense to me or consoles me. Charlie, my Rock of Gibraltar, who gives me unconditional love; who tunes in when no one else does or can; who gets upset when I'm upset; who gets upset when David and I argue; who is most happy when his family is together; who prefers love over food; who raises his paw when he wants something, mostly more stroking; who makes everyone laugh, even strangers; who makes me happy just to look at him; who loves me more than anyone else and shows it; who would fight to the death to protect me; is tired now.

So this weekend, please, Charlie, feel better. At least get to the point where you can keep some food in you. For me, Charlie, please do that. I want you to keep going and I want you to have more happy times. Fight Charlie. Please. Your mom loves you. Charlie knows that. "Mama's Boy," we call him — Charlie doesn't care. He's proud that he loves his mother like no other. Charlie makes my heart sing. Charlie's and my song is Frank Sinatra's "You Make Me Feel So Young" — "picking up all those forget-me-nots." Forget me not, Charlie. I will never forget you for as long as I live, maybe longer.

July 15, 2001

From the wee hours yesterday morning, David and I were busy with Charlie — first at the Brentwood Pet Clinic, then at North Bay Animal Emergency Hospital. Charlie had contracted pneumonia, on top of everything else. Tubes, IVs, oxygen. He couldn't move, could barely breathe. I was hysterical most of the day. Yet when we walked into the hospital early this morning, there was Charlie sitting up! And looking happy to see us. With him, in and around his open cage, was a little two-month-old gray kitten he was actually interested in. The sight of him sitting up and watching that kitten was so wonderful, so amazing. It made me feel a bit lighter. We learned the kitten had been abandoned. I wish we could have taken it home, but we're already dealing with so much.

So today Charlie's slightly better, but he still has to stay in the hospital. I went home on breaks so I wouldn't lose plants for lack of water. It's mid-July and hot. Speed-watered yesterday and this morning, then back to the hospital, to be with Charlie.

July 16, 2001

Again so hard to concentrate on anything, with what's going on with my Charlie. His right lung, according to an X-ray taken this morning, looks worse than Saturday, when we first brought him to the vet. The weekend was a blur. We were at the animal hospital the whole time — it was round-the-clock Charlie. All I could do in the garden was water.

Tomorrow Jésus will be here, and I have lots for him to do, but it's hard to think about explaining it all to him. I'm so focused on Charlie. I want him to get better. I want my Charlie back.

July 17, 2001

Jésus was here this morning, but it was not a happy time for me in the garden — I was too preoccupied. Charlie's still not home. He's still being shuttled between the hospital and the clinic. He had a test on his stomach this morning, which made him throw up — breathing that in is probably how he got pneumonia in the first place. One of the vets at the clinic came up with a possible diagnosis related to Charlie's esophagus. That's not the answer.

So I did only what was really necessary in the garden. It's times like these I think I'm nuts to try and hand-water almost an acre of plants and trees. I had Jésus plant three Scotch brooms. But my heart wasn't in it. My Charlie is struggling. What does he want? I think he hates it in the hospital.

My dear Charlie. He still has his appetite, and he still lifts his paw for me and wags his tail a bit. There still are some good signs. But the ache I'm feeling is indescribable. Not even gardening can relieve it. For a few brief moments this morning I became interested in my garden, but within seconds I was back to thinking about Charlie.

I want him with me, outside, in nature. I want him to smell the grass, breathe the ocean air, and be with Barney (our three-year-old Golden) and Sabrina (our eleven-year-old Sheltie). I don't want him in antiseptic settings — hospitals are no places for animals or people. What does Charlie want now? To be with his family, his pack — after all, he is alpha dog.

July 18, 2001

So last night in the hospital Charlie barked and barked until someone sat with him. He also pulled his catheter out. Charlie wanted to come home. And, not coincidentally, as I was driving to my office after being with him during the day, I thought: I want Charlie home. It's enough with hospitals and doctors and tests and IVs and X-rays. I want to see my Charlie in my garden. I want him walking in the grass, sitting under the Canary Island pines, breathing the fresh air. Charlie will heal better there.

So I guess Charlie made it happen: in the wee hours of the morning, he came home. He's still coughing, and the vet sent an arsenal of instructions and medications with him, but he's home. The reunion was great. Barney spun around in circles and practically wagged his tail off. Charlie sniffed him as if he were checking to make certain it was really Barney. They kissed one another. Sabrina watched intently.

Charlie was so happy. He bounced right into the house. He rolled on his back. He ran outside to the garden, sniffing everything and then relieving himself. It was such a heartwarming sight; it felt as if things were right again in the house. And it was so good to see him prance around the garden. I did not care what plants he trampled on. I had my Charlie back.

After all the excitement and hellos, Charlie settled into his bed and rested. I left the sliding glass door open a crack, so he could breathe the fresh air, and sat with him to make sure he was okay. I hope that, soon, his chest will be clear. No going back to the hospital for him.

July 19, 2001

Seeing Charlie so excited yesterday reminds me of a year ago, when he came out of an hour-long surgery to remove a growth from one of his eyelids …

During the surgery, as I sat in the waiting room, I heard Charlie yelping. So I was expecting that afterwards he would be not only disoriented from the anesthesia but also in some pain and unhappy. But when the doctor opened the door, which was at the end of a long hallway, Charlie came flying out, and when he saw me, he ran past David and my cousin Myrna, wagging his tail, big smile on his face, straight to me. Totally focused, like a laser. The doctor looked amazed. We were too ...

July 20, 2001

I'm sitting on a sofa, with Charlie on his bed at my feet, Barney right next to me, and Sabrina on a rug next to Charlie. Originally, the sofa was Arthur's. In fact, we still call it "Arthur's sofa." Blue denim, very comfortable. We got it for him after a recliner he had been sitting in was just about in shreds. I remember the day the sofa arrived. Charlie was about five years old ...

For weeks we had talked about the sofa coming. On the big day, two burly guys carried it down into the dogs' room. I made a fuss, saying it was Arthur's sofa. Arthur got all excited, but as the guys took the plastic covering off, lo and behold, it was Charlie who jumped up — Arthur just stood there. So I told Charlie it was Arthur's sofa and scooted him off. Then Arthur jumped up, plopped himself in the corner of the sofa near the big picture window, and from that moment on, the sofa was his. For the most part, when Arthur was on it, Charlie left him alone ...

Arthur

The garden looks so lovely now, with the sun going down. The tall Canary Island pines in the center, with the sun filtering through their long, thin needles. The potted ficus trees under them, their deep green surrounded by bright-green asparagus ferns. The big guava tree just to the right, surrounded by tea trees, their petals in varying shades of pink and white. And so many grasses and varieties of bamboo, all over the garden. I love how graceful and elegant they look, particularly through the soft lighting. I think this is my favorite time of day.

Thank God my Charlie is pulling through his pneumonia. Last Saturday morning, he couldn't stand, wouldn't eat, and had a temperature of 105. I ached. Awful feeling. I just wanted Charlie to be all right — nothing else mattered. David and I even slept in our car in the hospital parking lot from two until six in the morning. The whole thing seems surreal now.

So my Charlie's getting better and better, and now last weekend seems like a hundred years ago. I hated seeing him lying in a hospital, on IVs and oxygen. The whole week I'd been imagining Charlie walking around in my garden. Thankfully, I got my wish, and nothing could make me happier.

Charlie and me, playing on the patio

Four

July 22, 2001

A week ago I was watching Charlie fight for his life. Now, I'm sitting outside a yoga workshop in the Pacific Palisades, taking a lunch break in the sun. There are birds singing, tall trees everywhere, mostly pine, and the temperature is mild. Extraordinary day.

I'm sure it feels even more extraordinary because Charlie is pulling through his pneumonia. Last week he was struggling to breathe, with a tube of oxygen in his nose. And what is the yoga teacher concentrating on today? Breathing, just breathing in and out. The craziness of life.

Charlie strolled all through my garden this morning, and I followed him. I could tell how much he loved being home. He was practically skipping. So good to see. He was far ahead of me before he suddenly realized it, stopped, and looked around. He's hard of hearing, so I said, "Charlie," loudly. He spun his head, gave me a big smile. Then he came almost running over, and we continued on. I love to see him walking on all the paths I've created, sniffing the new plantings, relieving himself wherever he wants. Brings me such joy. Keep taking deep breaths, Charlie.

July 24, 2001

Today I sat on the lawn with Charlie. We were practically on top of each other — Charlie likes to be touching. Me too. We sat for the longest time. It was one of the few times I can remember just sitting in my garden, even though there are so many places to sit in it. We were at the top of the hill under the Canary Island pines, Charlie sniffing the air, looking all around, not letting me stop petting him. If I stopped, he raised his paw. It felt so good to be there with him.

Clear blue sky, slight breeze, warm, sitting in the shade under the pine trees, seeing Charlie so totally content breathing the fresh air. I could cry just remembering.

July 26, 2001

I worked in the garden for about four hours this morning, but it was with a very heavy heart. Charlie's doing much better, and for that I'm grateful, but he still doesn't have a lot of energy. That's so unlike the Charlie I've known, who is usually so eager and enthusiastic. I look into Charlie's eyes, and while I love doing that, I see how tired he is, I see all of his twelve years. My old guy. So odd. I've seen it a few times. For most of their lives they seem so young, and then they have an event, and in a matter of a week or so they seem older.

How Charlie feels colors everything. We sat in the garden for a while, and I petted him, but he did not seem happy. He just wanted to be in the house, on the sofa — I had to coax him outside. Maybe a B-12 shot will help.

So many things are wrong with Charlie, but his appetite and will are tremendous, and he's happy most of the time. And according to one veterinarian, his heart has a good, steady beat.

July 30, 2001

I'm looking forward to gardening with Jésus tomorrow. I want him to plant some papyrus grasses around the mint green wood bench in the middle of the garden. I've wanted to plant them there for a long time. They're long, eight feet high or so, green-stemmed, with clusters of string-like grass on top, delicate, and need lots of water. I also want him to take some ornamental grasses out of the ground and put them in pots. They're being overrun by African daisies, which are all over the garden and have eucalyptus and myoporum leaves in them that need to be cleaned out. A pine tree and a bottlebrush tree need to be transplanted, so they get more sun. And on and on.

In the center of the garden

I'm lucky I have such a simple activity that makes me happy. So comforting. But it's not the sitting in the garden — it's the caring for it, the tension leaving my body as I work, momentarily distracted, absorbed and content. It's the planting in the exact right spot. It's finding the perfect pot for the new plant. It's watching the plants grow and flourish. It's reviving a plant that looks to be on its last leg. It's the cultivating, the watering, the pruning, the raking. So grounding and centering.

I wish Charlie could be out in the garden with me. He's got to be watched, so maybe this weekend I'll bring his bed out.

CHARLIE

Lots of planting today. Jésus worked really hard, as usual. It's amazing how much he can get done in a day. He's in his twenties, is very strong, loves gardening, and so, not surprisingly, is already a master gardener. He's been working on our property for a little over a year and treats our garden like his own. Doesn't say much, just keeps on working.

Today, besides the papyrus grasses, the pine tree, and the bottlebrush tree, Jésus planted five Mexican marigolds, whose many stems have small dark green leaves and wonderful yellow-gold daisies. They also have a strong lemon-musk scent that I love. Even when just lightly brushed, they're very fragrant. I probably have forty of these plants in various places, providing bursts of color all over the garden.

Jésus planted the marigolds along a path across from a huge ficus benjamina and our sequoia, which is becoming a giant. Now I realize sequoias are some of the tallest trees on earth, so I don't know what I was thinking when I planted ours — every time I look at it, it seems to have grown.

I also planted a lavatera, an evergreen shrub that produces silk-like lavender flowers year-round, and a blue hibiscus — which is really light purple — that can get leggy if it's not pruned regularly. I must remember that. A blue wood table sits between the lavatera and the hibiscus along that same meandering path leading to the sequoia. Nice arrangement.

While Jésus was busy planting in the ground, I was busy planting in pots. Five big pots of angel vine. Sometimes called wire vine, it has wiry stems covered with very small leaves that quickly climb out of their pots and all over tables, chairs, and other plants. An easy plant, delicate-looking yet prolific.

I also potted two five-gallon Mexican weeping (otatea) bamboo, which have long thin leaves that are a lush, bright, almost chartreuse green. It's a rare plant and my favorite bamboo. I have many of them in the ground and in pots in various places throughout the garden. It's whimsical and lyrical, and in coastal areas such as Malibu, once it's established in the ground, it does not require much water — which is amazing, considering how lush it is.

I put together three big pots of little white-and-pink Santa Barbara daisies. They're also delicate-looking yet prolific, and once established, they're drought-tolerant and almost always blooming, attracting bees and butterflies. I love the way they look in the ground and overflowing in pots. They too add a whimsy.

August 3, 2001

Worked all day in the garden, didn't talk to anyone except Jésus. That put me in such a good mood. In the sun, with my beautiful plants and trees, smelling earth. Most everything watered, content. After all the rearranging and angling of plants, I have a sense of accomplishment. It's the first time in a long while that I remember being so totally distracted. The soft greens, the different shades of lavender, all the brightly colored bougainvillea — plants are dancing in my head as the day turns into evening and I bid my garden a good night. Can't wait to get up in the morning and see all the changes.

August 8, 2001

A garden seems frivolous now. My Charlie, my beautiful Charlie, has to lose his left eye. The melanoma that he got in his eyelid a year ago has come back. A few days ago I noticed something in the corner of his eye, and now it's getting bigger every day. An ophthalmologist says that without taking that eye out, Charlie would most likely have only a few months to live. I can barely stand thinking about it. My Charlie, with only one eye. All I want for the next few days is to be with Charlie. This morning he was lying on his back, with the green frog toy in his mouth, feet in the air, and so happy. I'm so scared and upset. Our birthday, Charlie's and mine, is on Sunday. I love you, Charlie. My garden is very far away.

August 9, 2001

I spent the day mostly with Charlie — I took off from work and only watered a little. I'm still trying to comprehend what I learned yesterday. Watering my garden helped to calm me somewhat, get me out of myself. But why can't Charlie just run and play and then simply bid us adieu? Why does he have to go through all these struggles?

David took pictures of Charlie and me in the garden this afternoon. I wanted pictures of Charlie's beautiful face before his eye is removed. People, even strangers, have often commented on how handsome his face is. I love Charlie so much. Tomorrow I want more pictures of Charlie in my garden. And Saturday even more.

In three days it's our birthday. At least I have him for his twelfth, and for that I am very thankful. I'm thankful for all the wonderful years, but of course I want more.

David and I are standing on our heads now for Charlie. We're both researching extensively, talking with doctors all across the country — as far away as Massachusetts. Anything to get a little more information to guide us. Is there any option other than removing his eye? How would losing his eye affect him, physically and emotionally? What are the risks of surgery, given his age and the type of surgery? The general consensus: The type of melanoma Charlie has is very aggressive, the surgery is essential to prolonging his life, despite the risk, and dogs with only one eye adjust very well.

Charlie's and my birthday has taken a far back seat now. And in the garden, I'm only watering. Now there is nothing more important than Charlie, wanting more time with Charlie and more pictures of Charlie, in the garden.

Charlie and me, days before his eye surgery

August 10, 2001

Little bit of watering this morning, because of the heat. That's about all I can get to, both physically and psychologically. So troubled about Charlie. How much I do not want his eye to be removed, how much I don't want him to suffer. I don't want his face to be changed forever. Is there some way to stop this? Is there something we are missing? Is there time to do more research?

The melanoma is growing as I write this; it's much bigger today than yesterday. My mind is consumed by Charlie. I just want my Charlie to be okay, I wish he would be okay. I wish he would not have to lose his eye.

August 11, 2001

A day before Charlie's and my birthday. Early this morning, David surprised me with a princess plant — deep-purple flowers. Tomorrow I hope to go to Calvin's Nursery in Malibu and get more plants for my birthday. And then spend the rest of the day with Charlie. It's getting closer to the day of the surgery to remove his eye. The ultimate purpose of the surgery is to prolong his life — I must keep that in mind. Life can be so hard sometimes, such terrible dilemmas.

My Puppy. Happy Twelfth Birthday, Charlie. You must pull through your surgery. We must spend more time together. Our birthday is hard this year.

But we all spent some lovely hours today in the garden. David took more than one hundred pictures, mostly of Charlie. More pictures tomorrow. More pictures of Charlie's beautiful face.

In the garden, the day before Charlie's twelfth birthday

Charlie, talking with his paw

CHARLIE

August 12, 2001

Sunday. Our birthday, Charlie's and mine. I love that we're born on the same day, but the surgery is two days from now, so it's hard to celebrate. I'll be his seeing eye person. Today, nearly the whole family — Charlie, Barney, Sabrina, David, and I (everyone but our cat Pippin) — spent some more hours in the garden. Charlie relaxed on a big rug, Barney played ball, David took pictures, I posed with Charlie, and Sabrina watched.

David and I spent about an hour at Calvin's Nursery. Casey and Randy, our friends and the nursery's owners, gave me a white orchid for my birthday. So sweet. For a moment I got lost in picking out plants: feather grasses, a snowbush, some asparagus ferns, bamboos, sweet pea bushes, agapanthus, lavenders, and more. That gave me a little relief from the overwhelming sadness I feel about my magnificent Charlie losing his eye, but my heart was still so heavy.

When the car had been packed — the trunk, the floors, and the back seat — and with the orchid on my lap, we made our way home. All my new plants sit on the patio, waiting to find their way into the garden. Wonderful birthday presents, all those plants. Gave Charlie lots of biscuits. Happy Twelfth Birthday, my sweet Charlie. I'd give away my entire garden if you could keep your eye.

August 13, 2001

I potted plants this morning, many that I bought yesterday. That felt good. I also tried to get current with the watering — nearly impossible these days, with the heat, and with everything that's going on with Charlie. Tomorrow is the surgery to remove his left eye. So hard to believe that's going to happen, but I have to take my chances with the surgery. Not even my garden can calm me — there's a constant hysteria inside me. This is a situation with no good alternatives.

Earlier in the day, I went out to do some errands. In the center of Malibu, a woman in her thirties was holding the hand of a little five- or six-year-old boy. In the boy's other hand was a long white-and-red cane. The little boy appeared to be blind. I thought of my little boy. At least he gets to keep his other eye, he's had twelve years of seeing with both eyes, and this is happening to him toward the end of his life. But those thoughts only consoled me a little.

Charlie, please pull through this. Dr. Olds, who has operated on Charlie three other times, as recently as five weeks ago, has agreed to do the operation.

CHARLIE

August 14, 2001

Charlie's surgery was this morning. Had his eye and the surrounding tissue taken out. He's home now, came through like a champ. David and I were at the clinic for the surgery and stayed with Charlie as he woke up. Dr. Olds let us have our own room and came in periodically to check on us. I had to go to work about two in the afternoon, but David stayed with Charlie the whole time.

August 15, 2001

Sat with Charlie on the sofa for the entire day. He slept, I read. He's doing well. His strength and stoicism remind me of that time in 1991 when Charlie injured the growth plate in one of his legs, roughhousing with Mandy. Charlie was about a year and a half then. That injury required a three-hour surgery to insert a big metal rod, followed by a grueling, nine-week recuperation. Stoic? Understatement. Charlie barely whimpered the entire time, despite the metal rod running through his leg. When he did show some signs of discomfort, such as not wanting biscuits, I brought him to Dr. Olds. He removed the rod immediately, saying that Charlie must have been in a lot of pain.

Charlie suffers quietly, more so than any being I've ever known.

Dr. Olds did a fantastic job. After a while, it became difficult to tell which back leg had been hurt. I know that that surgery has given Charlie a much better life. And it certainly showed, early on, what Charlie was made of.

August 16, 2001

I potted two new plants: a buddleja, known as the "butterfly bush" because it attracts butterflies, and a gypsophila, for the patio. Mostly I watched Charlie. He's doing really well. In fact, he got through the closed downstairs gate three times. I came out of the upstairs bathroom, and there he was, wagging his tail, after climbing two flights of stairs to get to me. My determined, loyal dog.

August 19, 2001

Truly the dog days of summer. Since June, we've been dealing with one health problem after another with Charlie. I have been so focused on him that it's been difficult to think of anything else. At work, I had to concentrate so hard to be present in each session, though I think ultimately that effort helped me, particularly because working with my patients is so soul-satisfying.

And my garden got completely overshadowed. Ah, to have the

luxury now of being able to wander through it and prune and rake for a couple of hours.

Life takes such funny twists and turns, and sometimes the turns are so sharp and quick, with very little room for error. That Charlie had to have his eye removed was such a shock, and in that state of mind David and I had to think so quickly and clearly about what was best for Charlie.

Now Charlie is recovering, again. Has his enthusiasm back. Amazing. On Tuesday he had almost two hours of surgery — we practically carried him home. Today, just a few days later, he's acting like it never happened.

Charlie and me, a week after his eye surgery

September 1, 2001

Thank God Charlie is a little more stable. I feel so much better when he feels better. Attached at the hip. I love when Charlie and I sit on the rug outside in the middle of the garden. We did that the day before his surgery, and I trimmed, very thoroughly, three grasses in pots. I wanted that moment to last. No surgery, nothing. Just Charlie and I in the garden, sitting together, and I would trim those grasses forever. I wanted to protect him from the surgery, from having to lose his eye. I couldn't. It's a week later. The surgery went fine. My Charlie has only one eye. And I remember that day and that feeling and Charlie and the grasses. And time, that can't stand still.

September 2, 2001

Charlie's doing so much better — in fact, he's better than he's been in years. His coat is much fuller, and he has a little bounce to his step. Early last evening I was watering, and out he came from the house, enthusiastic and wagging his tail. He's come through so much. That he doesn't have one eye is so difficult for me. But my Charlie is back. He and I sit out in the garden regularly now. I sit on a big rug under the Canary Island pines, he sits in my lap. I hold him and hug him and pet him, and I look at my garden with my Charlie in my lap, and all's right with the world, again.

Five

September 6, 2001

The season is changing, just like that. Fall's in the air. I love this time of the year. The promise of good times to come.

It's now so overcast and moist that I've been given a slight break with the watering, did only a tiny bit. It feels like I can catch my breath.

The pampas grasses are producing more and more of their elegant plumes. Huge clumps of very tall grass, with these magnificent plumes. So dramatic. I love watching them appear. Many of the plumes start off an extraordinary mauve color, with a texture like silk, and then, as they open, turn to cream and then beige.

Pampas grasses, in the garden

Raked some this morning, of course. There are so many huge trees on our property — eucalyptus, pine, myoporum — that there's always some raking to do. But I enjoy doing it. Like watering, like all aspects of gardening, it calms me and makes me happy. It's been that way since I was a very young girl, with my mother in her garden …

My mother loved plants, loved to garden. And like her mother, she had a green thumb. Our house was in West Los Angeles, across the street from Howard's Nursery, which is no longer there but at the time was very well-known. My mother would go there regularly, and starting at age four I would go with her. I can still see it: rows and rows of healthy plants and trees. She would eagerly pick out what she wanted, so quickly I could hardly keep up with her. She was happy there. I was too.

At home I would watch carefully as she tended her garden, both of us barefoot. It was so exciting to watch her plant and then see the plants get bigger and more beautiful. Many times, neighbors would bring over what looked like potted sticks for my mother to revive. In a short while, invariably and like magic, where there used to be just brown, there would be green. Fond memories ...

September 19, 2001

One week and a day after the monstrous terrorist attack. Our country is still reeling from it, and will be, I believe, for a very long time. I think it will be remembered as one of the darkest days of modern human history. How unlucky those people were whose lives were taken that day.

Sometimes it's physically hard to swallow when I think of the horrible events of last Tuesday. That people — it's hard to call those terrorists people — want to destroy life, spend their lives in training to destroy life, is beyond my comprehension. But then I think that out of the devastation in New York, Washington, and Pennsylvania will come a stronger national character. That we'll all have to grow up a little more. Life is change. Such an event shines a beacon on one's life, changes priorities. It has made me realize how lucky I am to have my Charlie back in the garden, walking around picking up twigs. I'm so thankful, even though he's missing an eye.

So I will continue to garden. I will continue my psychotherapy practice. I will continue to take my dogs for walks. I will forge ahead with my life, just like Charlie. And just like Charlie, I will never give in.

Six

November 10, 2001

Spent about an hour in the garden, mostly with Charlie, Barney, and Sabrina. Charlie sat in my lap, Barney played ball, and Sabrina sat right next to me. Pleasant.

It's so wonderful to see and feel my Charlie healthy. His fur is fuller and thicker than I've ever seen. He's got so much energy, and the place where his eye used to be has just about healed. I'm so grateful. Sitting in the garden with Charlie in my lap is the best feeling in the world. In July I thought it was all over. Now it's November, and it's a whole new day.

December 4, 2001

One of those spectacular days. Blue sky, crisp air, clear enough to see forever. Invigorating. From the upstairs deck, I can see the Pacific Ocean through the Canary Island pines. Jésus was here today, worked really hard at cultivating, cleaning, and pruning. He did a fantastic job.

And my Charlie, whose heart and personality are bigger than the Empire State Building, is now regularly running around the garden. Even his back seems a lot better. Once again, he's looking for twigs to chew and is always really proud of himself when he finds one. He has to be protective of the twigs because if Barney sees one, he tries to take it out of Charlie's mouth. Dogs.

December 24, 2001

It's the night before Christmas, and I have a bunch of new plants. Went to Montecito with David. First stop: Pan's Garden in Summerland. I bought lots of little plants in one-inch and two-inch containers, also two five-gallon eugenias, and a shiny maroon gazing ball. It was good seeing Rob and John, the owners — Merry Christmas to all. The energy is so wonderful this time of year. Why can't people be this happy and kind, and look each other in the eye and smile, all year long?

From there it was straight on to Turk's Nursery in Montecito, where I bought five more eugenias, four Mexican marigolds, and some feather grasses, all in one-gallon containers. I also bought two beautiful chartreuse cypress trees in five-gallon containers. I never think I'm going to get as many plants as I do, but I just can't seem to resist. David was a good sport, as usual, and piled them in his car.

David's not a gardener. He's from New York and grew up in

Manhattan, so he didn't see too much gardening. But he appreciates the garden I've created, even does some pruning. He's very artistic — writes poetry, among his many talents — so the pruning always looks great. Besides, he's an actual genius. He's one of those people who knows just about everything and can solve just about any problem — MIT graduate, master's and bachelor's degrees. His line of work is far from the garden: computer consultant.

David came to Los Angeles around 1980. A few years later, he moved into an apartment in the same four-unit condominium on the beach in Malibu that I'd been living in for more than two years. He's told me that what first attracted him to me was how lovingly and attentively I cared for my dog Simon, a Cairn Terrier mix who was ten years old at the time. And my attraction to David was also related to Simon. On one of our first dates, which was supposed to be a nice drive up the coast to Santa Barbara, I didn't want to go, because Simon didn't feel well. David stayed with me the whole day while I cared for Simon and was very understanding and supportive.

David with Pippin, our cat

It's early evening as I write this. David is bringing in all the plants from the car. And I'm sitting with my Charlie in my lap. Sabrina, my gorgeous, smart-as-a-whip Sheltie, is at my feet. Barney, my filled-with-life young Golden, is staring at me, in the hope I will do the thing he loves the most: throw him the ball. Charlie continues to sleep in my lap, lifts his paw occasionally to remind me to pet him.

It truly is a Merry, Happy Christmas. No fancy parties, just the warmth of my wonderful family, and the garden I will tend in the morning.

December 28, 2001

A little miracle in the garden today. This morning my favorite potted otatea bamboo was brown and twiggy. It had been so gorgeous, so green and full. I remember the day I bought it at Turk's Nursery not that long ago. I was so happy to bring it home. Well, yesterday was quite hot and very windy, and the bamboo had not been watered for a day. Just one day! I was so upset. So I watered it and watered it and watered it. I had very little hope. I thought about moving it someplace where I would not have to look at it. And I thought about how long, if ever, it would take to bring it back to where it was. Should I cut it back and take the brown dead stuff off? One day without water — it was that fragile, and what had happened to it was my fault. I soaked it — and every other potted plant.

And then, oh only about three hours later, as I walked by the plant (almost afraid to look, but I did), I saw lots of green. I couldn't believe it! Amazingly, it appeared to have come back to life. Seems it had pulled itself in, I guess to conserve its energy in the dry heat and wind, and so it had only looked dead. I was so happy that it revived itself when it got water. Such intuitive intelligence.

2002

Charlie

Seven

April 27, 2002

I spent most of the morning and the early afternoon gardening.
Potting new plants, watering of course — still no rain — and pruning.
A mild temperature. The garden looks beautiful. I like to think of
it as a cottage garden. Lots of plants and trees, close together, not
formal, plants seeding themselves, and lots of color. Abundant,
fragrant, and colorful. And filled with birds and butterflies.

About two months ago, a male robin redbreast was singing
at the top of his lungs on the upstairs balcony. Day after day he
would be there. He seemed to be having the greatest time. Soon
I started seeing two robins, the second not as brightly colored as
the first — a female. Together, flying back and forth carrying twigs,
they built their nest in an old wreath that was hanging on an outer
wall of our house, over the upstairs deck off the living room. That
spot is one of the least-frequented of our house. When their nest
was finished, the female stayed in the nest for some time, most
likely to sit on the eggs.

Finally, I started hearing squawking, particularly in the early
mornings. I tried to stay away so as not to disturb them. It sounded

as if there were thirty birds in there. What a racket! An adult bird would fly in and out regularly. Then one day, I guess about a week and a half ago, I saw a little baby bird standing on the edge of the nest — just standing, with eyes closed. Adorable. It would be just a matter of time before this little guy would take off.

It's been quiet the last couple of days: no adults, no babies, no squawking. It was wonderful having those sweet sounds of new life at our house. What a great way for spring to arrive. I didn't even mind being careful about not getting too close to the deck. I miss them. I wonder where they all went. Are they okay? No choice but to let go.

May 12, 2002

I was busy in the garden all day today but still was able to do only about half of what I'd originally planned. It was fun, but toward the end I was tired. I think all the watering is taking a toll. But then I look at the garden and it's so beautiful, and you can't have that kind of beauty without some work. So I'll learn to take the watering in stride, and anyway, it won't always be so sunny. I'm constantly reminding myself that things change.

Speaking of change, it was about a year ago that we started our marathon of illnesses with Charlie. A year! But there we were this afternoon, Charlie and I, lying on the sofa together, cuddling. He looks great, lots of energy, lots of enthusiasm. As usual, he would raise his paw if I stopped petting him. And me, I was just as content, if not more so. A year ago I never would have guessed that he and I would have this time together. Lying there with Charlie today, on Mother's Day, was the best present I could have had.

July 11, 2002

Seven thousand pounds of pink-peach-colored Arizona flagstone was delivered this morning, along with five thousand pounds of sand in which to place the stones. That should be enough stone for all the new pathways I want to create. A truck with a forklift delivered all the stones and sand to the driveway. Incredibly, with just a wheelbarrow, Jésus brought it all into the garden today — it took him six hours. Slow, steady Jésus: he stays with it until he gets the job done. Although it was hot and humid today, he just kept at it. I told him to take some breaks, but he didn't seem to want to. Then I had to go to work. I presume he ate lunch. I couldn't believe it when I got home and saw that all the stone and sand had been brought in. Where do you find people like Jésus?

August 11, 2002

Got a notion in my head this morning about needing pots. Soooo, off to Summerland and Pan's Garden. Everything there was at least forty percent off, which resulted in lots of pots, mostly terra cotta, and lots of plants too. It was so much fun piling them all in the car. I love thinking about which plants to put in which pots, all the possibilities.

Right now I'm thinking about Charlie's and my birthday, which is in less than two hours. Happy Birthday, Charlie, my glorious Golden Retriever, almost thirteen years old. You pulled through a million problems last summer. At times, it seemed, defying gravity.

I definitely got my Charlie back. How lucky. We get to celebrate another birthday together.

Eight

August 18, 2002

For the past few days our beautiful Sabrina has had a bad kidney infection. She's been in the hospital since Friday. She's on an IV antibiotic drip and not eating, so she's very anemic. I was at the hospital most of the day. I'm so sad.

Seems like just a few minutes ago that David rescued Sabrina, from the streets of downtown Los Angeles, but actually it was six and a half years ago ...

David called me at work at eleven in the morning and told me he had found a Sheltie. She had been walking alongside a very busy street, huge trucks barreling along in both directions. She was very dirty and had no identification. Besides David's devotion to dogs, he had had two Shelties years ago that he adored. So I pretty much knew something was going to come of this, even though we had three dogs already.

When I came home that night, she was in the grooming truck getting ready to have a bath. The groomer had come over at eight in the evening especially for her. She was a mess — her coat was matted and gray — but through all that I saw a twinkle in her eyes.

The groomer worked on her for a long time, and when he was done she looked like a princess. She was a big, gorgeous Sheltie, with incredible markings: a full white ruff, a perfect face, with white on her forehead coming down to and around her nose, and a thick mahogany coat. Just like, David said, the Shelties you'd find in Britain. We could picture her herding sheep in the Shetland Islands.

Sabrina

David and I sat at the kitchen table while she was being groomed and tried to figure out what to do. Do we keep her? It was about a two-minute discussion. She stays. Now, how do we introduce this little princess to our three big dogs? We brought Mandy, Arthur, and Charlie out to the grooming truck. They each jumped in, sniffed around, and jumped out. Sabrina just stared at them.

When the grooming was done, we brought her into the house. Mandy loved her right away — someone else to play with. They had so much fun together, running and roughhousing. But Arthur was a little uppity with Sabrina. It took him two weeks to get used to her, and she never forgave him for that. Never forgot. She would snap at him when there was food around. She would bark at him when he entered a room. It was so funny to watch: here was this big male Afghan, intimidated and respectful of this little street urchin Sheltie. She seemed to have him coming and going.

Charlie responded by being protective of Sabrina. And she was very respectful of him, simply fell in love. If he was sitting someplace, she would have to sit right next to him, even if the area was cramped. She deferred to him and followed him. Charlie was her guy. And Charlie seemed to like the attention. With her support, Charlie had more clout in the pack, even though before Sabrina he had been the youngest. They were and are cute together. I started calling them Mr. and Mrs. Puppy, after one of Charlie's names.

Charlie and Sabrina

Sabrina fit right in, was so intelligent she knew exactly how to relate to each of us. You could see her thinking in her eyes. Assess, analyze, evaluate, just like the classic Sheltie. Went on constantly, still does …

Oh Sabrina, how hard your life must have been on the streets. I felt so good taking you in and giving you a great home and a great life. Please feel better, my Princess Sabrina Brittany Lampert.

August 26, 2002

Sabrina is back from the hospital, but far from better. The doctor thinks the routine should be twelve hours on fluids at the hospital and twelve hours at home, for five days. My beautiful, fearless little girl. She was so happy to be home, and Charlie and Barney were so happy to see her. But I haven't heard her bark in over a week. She normally barks incessantly, though David says she's quiet for a Sheltie. I miss all the barking. I'll never complain about that bark again.

You would think I would get used to the deal with dogs — their lives are short. Far too short. Why do I think that will change? I hate that they get sick, and it pains me so much to see them struggle. You'd think I would stop getting dogs, but of course I won't. I thought maybe having a number of dogs would make it easier when one would get sick. Nope. Just as bad. I still ache as much for the sick one.

What about getting a parrot? Would I get as attached? They can live a hundred years or more. Well, then, that presents the problem of this being living longer than me. Who would I will it to, and how much money would I leave for it? All this is giving me a headache. Time for bed, before I pass out from exhaustion, trying to solve an insolvable problem.

August 29, 2002

Hot August days. Lots of watering, particularly all the potted plants, of which there are hundreds. Sabrina was home all day today. So good to have her home. I'm sick: sore throat. Oh well.

August 30, 2002

Looks like Sabrina is doing a little better. Please keep going, Sabrina. We all love you and want you with us lots longer. We're all pulling for you. We'll do everything we can to support those kidneys. My little street urchin. She's fighting so hard. Two solid weeks of back and forth to the hospital. My big girl, brave girl. I love saying that to her.

Tomorrow Jésus will be here. Saturday, all day. I'm a little under the weather, but I think I will be able to get out and garden. I know that will make me feel better. Healer, heal thyself.

Nine

September 2, 2002

Was going to write when I got home last night, but instead, I came home to find my Charlie unable to stand. I went into shock. David and I had gone to a movie. It was the first time we'd done anything fun in two weeks, and we weren't even gone that long. When we walked into the house, Charlie was upright and happy to see us. Next thing I know, he's on the floor, unable to get up. David had to carry him outside the house. He was like a Raggedy-Ann doll.

Oh God. Not yet, Charlie. Don't go yet. Don't go ever.

So David stood him up. Charlie couldn't even walk to the lawn. David carried him back inside. I was hysterical and telling Charlie to fight. He looked so tired. Did he have a heart attack? I took his vitals: all good. Temperature was normal. We called North Bay Animal Emergency Hospital, but then decided to let him rest instead of taking him there. I kept stroking him. He was pretty unresponsive, though he did drink water. Periodically he would look at me.

What's going on? First Sabrina. Now Charlie. It's too much. So

I just lay with him. For hours.

Then, thankfully, he started looking a little better — his gums got a little pinker, and he became a little more responsive. David picked him up to go out. Ah, Charlie walked on his own, went into the garden to relieve himself. He seemed happier.

That night, we all slept downstairs: me on the sofa; Charlie on a dog bed right next to me, so my arm could touch him; David on a dog bed; Barney at my feet at the end of the sofa; and Sabrina near Charlie. By morning Charlie was lots better: smiling, rolling over, making eye contact. Wish I could figure out what's happening with him. Better yet, I'd love to hear what Charlie thinks. Maybe "I'm tired, I'm older, I've got some things wrong, but I love being here, so do what you have to do!" My Charlie. Worth his weight in Golden.

September 4, 2002

Got in some gardening this morning. Lots of watering, of course. But I also had time to pot some roses. They look good in pots, particularly varieties with a lot of color, such as double delight.

Sabrina continues to show some slight improvement, though she's still tired and foggy. She seems a little more alert today. I took her alertness for granted all these years. She was always so aware, so hyper-vigilant, so in charge, so on top of her game.

September 5, 2002

No, can't be! Listening to the vet, I almost wanted to tell him to stop talking. He had run an ultrasound on Charlie.

I had taken Charlie into the garden this morning, and there was a lot of blood in his urine. We went straight to the vet — we were there before eight. It turns out Charlie has stones in his bladder, heart disease, and tumors in his liver, adrenal glands, and in the main artery to his heart. There's more to it, but I stopped listening to the details. We can't do anything about all this, because he is thirteen years old and now apparently has a weaker heart.

None of this illness is showing. He's eager, enthusiastic, hungry, and filled with love. My big beautiful guy. I'm unbelievably scared and sad.

Dr. Olds so kindly told David that he will be there for all of us and will help us do what is best for Charlie. Dr. Robert Olds, a renowned orthopedic surgeon, is one of the great veterinarians. He's what you wish every doctor would be like. And he also has a dog named Charlie.

It was so difficult hearing this awful news today. There are so many things wrong with my Charlie. How can it be? It makes no sense to me. I think I'm still in shock.

Dr. Olds told David that we need to enjoy Charlie. He may just have a few months. Months! My Charlie, just months. Can't be. I refuse to believe that. Would it ever be enough time? No. Would thirty years be enough? No. I want Charlie to live forever.

CHARLIE

September 7, 2002

The days are a blur. My Charlie is leaving. My thirteen-year-old Golden. My big, noble Golden. I'm more than sad. This time it appears he's going for sure. I can't stand it, I love him so much. He lies in the middle of the doorway to the garden on a big round dog bed. Dr. Olds, who visited today, a Saturday, said that Charlie is going into a coma and will just go to sleep. It's a vigil now. I'm sick inside. To lose Charlie. It can't be. My buddy. My joy.

He breathes fast. His eyes are mostly closed. His body temperature is dropping. Please go easily and don't suffer, Charlie. His big heart is giving out. He's more than tired and only makes eye contact every once in a while. Mostly he lies there. Is this what you want, Charlie? I'm doing the best I can for you, Charlie. You deserve the best. You gave me so much: love, loyalty, attention, laughter. Oh, your funny ways. Backing up into my lap and then sitting. Or pressing up against my back while I'm on the floor in front of the mirror putting on makeup. Charlie. I'll miss you and all that you brought to my life.

And I hope I made your life as good as you made mine. I love you, my Puppy.

September 8, 2002

Awful time. My Puppy lies in his bed all day. Drinks some water or Tahitian noni juice from an eyedropper. We make some eye contact, but mostly he sleeps. I'm so incredibly sad to be losing him. My loyal friend. My great love. So we continue the vigil with him. I can't think to end it now. Maybe I'll get a sign. Maybe he'll go on his own. Or maybe, please maybe, he will rejuvenate himself and start all over again, as if thirteen years never happened. Maybe. Maybe. Maybe.

September 9, 2002

I can't believe it! Charlie actually ate some baby food, showed an interest in it! I loved seeing that. He hasn't stood up in four days, but I'm happy with the slightest improvement. Yesterday I thought it was all over. Today, I have some hope.

September 10, 2002

Incredibly, Charlie made a yip sound today! He was lying on his big round bed. I was sitting right next to him. Some contractor had come over to talk to me and was standing over Charlie and me when, out of nowhere, I heard Charlie yip. I couldn't believe my ears. How could that be? Charlie had neither walked in days nor made a sound. I think maybe he heard the man close to him and perhaps wanted to assert himself. Later he actually lifted his paw, wagged his tail, sat up a little, and ate seven jars of baby food. Seven! Amazing! And he seemed happy! I was thrilled.

Must go to sleep now. My Charlie is sleeping soundly. Deep sleep. Good nite, my beautiful Charlie!

September 11, 2002

September 11th. A year later. Infamous day.

At our house, the whole day had to do with Charlie. He had a much better day. That meant I had a much better day. David and I were busy with him all the time, changing his bedding, washing, drying, cooking, cleaning, cuddling with him, and so on. My big, full-steam-ahead Golden.

Well, my dear Charlie, as long as you fight to survive, I will do everything in my power to support you and fight for you. Bless your goodness, Charlie. Have I told you how happy you make me?

September 12, 2002

Joyous day. Charlie picked himself up this morning and walked! He stood himself up and walked! A miracle. Last week, according to Dr. Olds, he was heading into a coma, with just a few days to live. Incredible. Charlie tries with all his might.

This morning was fantastic, seeing him get up. I was watering and looked over and saw him casually walking. I dropped the hose and walked with him. I couldn't believe my eyes.

I had to go to work in the early afternoon, but I heard from David that Charlie took himself out and calmly walked around under the Canary Island pines. My boy.

Every day with him is precious to me now. He sleeps right next to me as I write this, his face twitching slightly. Guess he's having a dream. I want to celebrate, but I won't. I will just enjoy every minute that I have with Charlie.

Charlie, how much longer can I have you? Forever would be good.

September 13, 2002

My Charlie is doing extraordinarily well. Dr. Olds called tonight and, without even saying "hello" first, said, "I have a wish. If I get sick, I want to lie on that big round dog bed and have you take care of me. I know I would get better." I laughed. He also said he never would have guessed that Charlie would ever get up again.

I, of course, will never, ever take Charlie for granted. I will give him millions of kisses. I will breathe in his scent, the best dog scent I've ever known. I will make every one of his days happy. I will sing our song to him, "… picking up lots of forget-me-nots." I will give him as much love as he can stand. What an incredible, magnificent, miraculous, determined, tenacious, noble, big-hearted, strong-willed guy. David and I tend to him twenty-four hours a day — willingly. Because Charlie does not like to be left alone, one of us has to be in the room with him at all times. More and more, he is able to walk, his appetite is enormous, he throws his paw in the air and watches the goings on. Each day he is a bit better. Each day I feel a bit better. My Charlie. My comeback kid. Go figure. There is no rational explanation for what happened. It doesn't matter. My Charlie is coming back to me.

Ten

September 15, 2002

And so Charlie continues to improve. No way to explain his pulling out of a near-coma, but all that matters is that he feels better. And Sabrina looks like she's feeling better too. It's been a horrendous month. Please let everyone be well for a while.

It's Saturday, and Jésus was here all day. He dug basins around the plants to hold water, and he cultivated to aerate the soil. Then he watered. He did a wonderful job. What a relief to have so much help with the garden, today and three other days this week. Jésus does so many things well, and after today I can add watering to the list of his gardening abilities. I watched him with the hose. It seemed effortless. He was quick and covered so much ground. And it has been so good having his sweetness on the property, with the myriad of problems we've been dealing with. He is a gem of a person and a gem of a gardener. I've come to really appreciate his quiet, earnest energy.

Lots of gardening today. And lots of hugs and kisses to Charlie. I must seize these moments. So much is still precarious.

September 16, 2002

Speed watering. That's all I have time for these days. My time is divided between Charlie, Sabrina, and my work. Sabrina is stable. Charlie continues to do better and loves to eat. No, he is actually obsessed with eating. Bless his heart and stomach.

Today, while he was outside on his dog bed, I collected all the stipa grasses in little pots, trimmed them, and got the dead grass out. They start out so green and in a short time they look like beige feathers. It's a project I've been meaning to do for a while. Felt good doing it, especially with my Charlie right next to me. He slept through most of it. I loved seeing him so peaceful.

Time to go to sleep. For the past few weeks, David and I have been sleeping downstairs in the dogs' room, me on one of the dog beds, right next to Charlie. Sometimes I'll wake up and realize we're breathing the same air. I had been sleeping on the sofa, but it was hurting my back. The dog bed is much better. Must be near Charlie.

September 19, 2002

My Charlie isn't doing too well, again. His breathing is slow and his appetite is poor. He's still making eye contact, though, and he still wants Jan's Wow Bow Biscuits. What could they have in those biscuits? Oh my Charlie. I knew when he woke up this morning that he did not feel great. I hope he's not in pain. I hate going to work now. I don't know what I'll come home to, and all I really want to do is be with Charlie. Some responsiveness with his paw this morning, but not much. Please stay for a while, Charlie.

September 20, 2002

So relieved it's Friday. A few days of rest. Plus, I don't have to be at work wondering how Charlie and Sabrina are doing. Where are those carefree days of pruning, raking, designing, potting? Just about the only gardening I can do these days is watering, and I hardly even have time for that.

My Charlie continues to struggle. Last night he was very sick, upset stomach. David and I were cleaning him and the room at four thirty in the morning. For most of the day, fortunately, Charlie's been peaceful, but he doesn't look particularly happy. Maybe worn out from last night's activities. But he's eating. Such determination.

He's sleeping now. Periodically he wakes and looks up to see if I'm still sitting on the sofa. Charlie. His perfect name. Looked like a Charles when he was a puppy, but Charlie seemed to suit him more. Don't know exactly why. Guess Charles sounded too formal for him. There is no pretense with the name Charlie. And Charlie is the least pretentious being I know. Sleep well tonight, Charlie.

CHARLIE

September 21, 2002

It's Saturday. Jésus was here all day. He got a lot done, and helped me with the watering.

Charlie's a little sluggish — his stomach is still upset. My Puppy seemed to feel a little better at night, though. I'm so relieved.

September 22, 2002

Sunday. I felt so much better today, because Charlie felt better. He was happier, even wagged his tail a few times. Got up on his own a few times, drank water on his own, and in general had more energy. While I was sitting outside, he backed into my lap, lifted his paw many times, and made lots of eye contact.

And his stomach has settled down some. We're giving him a new diet that he loves: yams, barley — which David is grinding so that Charlie can digest it more easily — and a special canned food that's supposed to be good for his heart. All of which seems to be helping.

So I saw my Charlie again today. So much wrong with him, but his sheer will seems to be overriding everything. My miracle dog. Every day is a gift now, and I'm treasuring my time with him. A good day today. We were together for most of it. He sleeps so peacefully now. He's dreaming. His foot is moving. Such a change from yesterday.

Finally got to Calvin's Nursery today. It was good to be there, doing something besides worrying about Charlie. It must have been two months or so since the last time I was there. Went for soil, and of course wound up with a bunch of plants. I had so much fun potting them when I got home. It's been so long since I've potted anything. But I do know that with all that's going on, if I did not have my gardening I would be out of my mind. It helps that much.

September 24, 2002

Tuesday. Too bad I couldn't stay in the garden all day. Jésus was here from eight in the morning until four in the afternoon. He and I worked together until about eleven, after which I had to go in and get ready for work. Once again, I had to wrench myself out of the garden. I was so enjoying it, and it has been a long time since I've been able to do that. One thing that's helping tremendously is that my Charlie is feeling better and starting to act like his old self. Yes, a little older, a little slower, a little thinner, but that big spirit, that big generous, happy spirit, is emerging out of my Puppy again. Makes me feel so good to see that.

Got lots done in the garden today. Jésus planted some of my favorite shrubs: rock roses, gypsophilas, and Mexican marigolds. The rock roses add a softness to the garden — greenish-gray leaves with many little pink flowers. I have one fairly large area with a pathway of stepping stones running through it and lots of rock rose bushes on either side. I love walking there.

Jésus also planted two large ficus nitidas along the fence line, which is filled with them as well as other fast-growing, lush, tall trees: ficus benjaminas, podocarpus, and myoporum. Just about finished planting there — I'll bet Jésus is happy. He must have planted hundreds of trees along that fence line, doubling and tripling up in places. I started out a few years ago simply trying to privatize our house, which sits on a slight hill in the middle of several other houses on a cul-de-sac. I was just going to plant trees along the fence line and mix in some vines for color: red bougainvilleas, orange-flowered Cape honeysuckle, purple morning glories. But little by little I worked my way across the entire property, until almost an acre became filled with plants and trees.

Jésus moved some potted plants for me, tied some grasses, raked, and pruned. We're getting ready for winter, and there's a lot of pruning to do, particularly of the acacia and eucalyptus trees, which seem to grow like weeds.

A great vacation for me would be one week working in the garden with Jésus. That would be a wonderful gift. He is so easy to get along with, and we barely know each other's language. Who knows, maybe that's one of the reasons we work so well together. No matter, it was a good day.

In the garden with Jésus

September 25, 2002

Spent most of the day in the garden, had so much fun just playing. Potted eight new ornamental grasses, fertilized the potted roses (I have to put the fertilizer in deep so that the dogs don't get to it, little rascals), pruned the plumbago (got its blue petals all over me), moved the potted geraniums (I have no luck with geraniums in the ground), and of course watered. Just had an excellent time in my simple, quiet, natural, beautiful world. And Jésus will be here again tomorrow. What a treat.

Charlie is doing better, though still not out of the woods. But to go from heading into a coma three weeks ago to where he is now is amazing. He's eating voraciously, he's enthusiastic, he's getting up on his own, he's alert. And Sabrina's doing pretty well, considering the problems with her kidneys.

How I love dogs — they are so resilient and try so hard. And they're so stoic, some more than others, of course. Charlie, I think, is the most so. He just handles things. It's as if he makes the assumption that everything will be okay. And it usually is for Charlie. I could learn from him.

September 26, 2002

Short day in the garden. Jésus here for just four hours. I was out at about six thirty in the morning watering, but I had to come in at about nine thirty to get ready for work. Jésus cleaned up an area where a tree had been taken out. Then he planted five little myoporum, a fifteen-gallon ficus nitida, and an asparagus fern that was in a broken pot. And, of course, moved potted plants around for me.

Most important, my Charlie is getting better — rolling on his back, wagging his tail, getting back his enthusiasm for life. That's the best part of today.

September 28, 2002

Nighttime, slight mist in the air. Why doesn't it rain? We need a good downpour desperately. Poor Southern California.

September 30, 2002

My Charlie. My big guy. Last night I was sitting in my office at home, on the floor, doing my billing, papers all over — records, envelopes, the Diagnostic Code Manual. Then in walks my big Puppy. Thirteen years old, achy joints, stiff back, back legs not working great. But still he ambled on in, plopped himself in the middle of my papers, positioned himself so that he and I were touching, and proceeded to go to sleep. My heart melted. I moved my papers out from under him and arranged everything so that I could continue what I was doing. It felt so good to have him next to me. Charlie works hard to keep our connection going, alive and energized. What a dog.

Eleven

October 3, 2002

It makes me happy to prune and shape the palms in pots, which I did this morning, about seven of them. I got lost in doing it. Then I heard David letting the dogs out. They'd just eaten. I was snipping and cleaning, and out of the corner of my eye I saw a dog coming over to me. Of course, it was Charlie. I was in a dark, out-of-the-way place in the garden, at a corner of the property. Near the fence by the guesthouse. Charlie came over smiling, tail wagging gently. Happy with himself. Mission accomplished: I found my mom. I hugged him, I kissed him, I was warmed all over that he put in such an effort to find me. I stopped my cutting and trimming and walked with Charlie around the entire garden.

I treasure these days with him.

October 5, 2002

Saturday. I did what I said I would do: I worked all day in the garden. I'm like my young Golden, Barney. He's obsessed with the ball; I'm obsessed with the garden. We call him "ball brain." He's such a happy dog, particularly with a ball.

So it was one great day in the garden. Jésus was here all day, and we got so much done. Planted three new papyrus grasses, and took out four fountain grasses that were nearby and put them in pots. Planted the potted blue oat grasses (hope they take), three clovers, and two white cosmos.

Ornamental grasses in the garden

Jésus planted a few more Australian tea trees. We must have ten or more in various places. They're a graceful tree, with multiple twisting trunks and many branches, some weeping, with little gray-green leaves, and white flowers in the spring. Also planted several more sweet pea bushes — lots of green foliage and little purple flowers that are in bloom most of the year and attract butterflies and hummingbirds.

And while Jésus was planting asparagus ferns in the ground, I was planting some in pots. It looks like I can't have too many of these plants — I probably have about four hundred or more in various places all over the property. Sprays of small, needle-like, vibrant chartreuse leaves — my favorite color in the garden.

I also potted some agapanthus. I have many in the ground too. I love this plant, essentially a clump of long green leaves, with a long-stemmed large lavender/purple flower that starts blooming in the spring and stays in bloom for months. It also attracts hummingbirds.

Jésus put more Arizona flagstone in, wonderful paths of it. The next project is to plant in between the stones, but it's hard to figure out what to put there. I'm sure I will.

What a welcome relief, being in the garden all day. I had so much fun. Seems my troubles were on Pluto for the day. Between the light romantic comedy *Sweet Home Alabama* last night and the garden all day today, I feel much better.

Had my Charlie out with me a bit. He was content as long as I was within sight but would start barking if I wasn't. It was a beautiful day: blue sky, warm, and the garden was radiant. Tomorrow I hope to do more of the same. Simple pleasures.

A path in the garden

CHARLIE

October 13, 2002

Spent a lot of time with Charlie and Sabrina. Charlie is doing better, but Sabrina is really struggling. David is giving her subcutaneous fluids once or twice a day, and she's on medication and a special kidney diet. But the most recent tests show her kidneys are failing.

I do see Sabrina happy for moments during the day: She wags her tail, I hear her bark, and she loves to eat. This morning she wanted to sit outside with me and be petted — she sat right next to me for the longest time. I liked that. But it's hard watching her be so disoriented. Makes me sad. My little girl.

October 21, 2002

Overcast, gray, quiet morning. Odds and ends in the garden. Mostly attended to my two sick dogs — stomach problems. With Charlie, I think he'll be okay. He's happy, so I think this episode will pass. But I've been noticing lately that, though Sabrina's appetite is good, and her spirit is still strong, she seems more disoriented and is having trouble seeing and hearing. I love you, my little girl — I know you're leaving.

So it was hard to garden. I'm forcing myself, but I'm so sad. Sabrina, you have not been with us long enough. By some miracle, could you pull out of this?

November 4, 2002

Sabrina. My little Sheltie. She's lost so much weight, though she still wants to eat. And there still are times when she's perky. Brave little girl.

But my sadness and worry about her gnaw at me. I feel as though I'm living under a dark cloud. I don't want Sabrina to suffer.

November 6, 2002

Sabrina's gone. My little girl is gone. My feisty little girl. I'm so very sad. I was with her this morning while she was dying. Thank God I could be there with her then. I hope that made it easier for her. I stroked her little face. She went quietly. Collapsed on the lawn, lay there briefly, then she was gone. I closed her eyes. I cried.

Later that day, Charlie would go to the box that Sabrina was in, wag his tail, sniff, and then walk away. He was sad, except when he sniffed Sabrina. Barney walked back and forth a number of times from where she had died to the box, trying to understand what had happened, I think.

Sabrina was so sweet. I knew that about her for a long time. Oh, she would bark incessantly about food, be pushy when it was around, and try to control the other dogs. She would snap at Barney when he was playing ball. But underneath all that aggressive behavior was that sweet girl, with those angel eyes. I loved looking into them. We would lock eyes and exchange love.

Sabrina, I hope you had a great life with us. I wanted it to be beyond your wildest expectations, because of your hard time on the streets. I hope that it was. We loved having you with us. You perfectly-marked Sheltie.

Sabrina, I loved that after four years you decided to trust me enough to bond with me. I loved how carefully you would watch me and listen to me. I loved taking you on walks and out in public. You were always so appropriate. Where did you come from? And how old were you? I'm not sure. A little mystery girl. Princess Sabrina Brittany Lampert. Rest in eternal peace, my Sabrina. I have you in my heart. I came to love you a lot.

November 7, 2002

I miss Sabrina. I see that perky little face all over. Those intelligent eyes. Today, I imagined her sitting in back of me in the living room while I was sitting on the floor in front of the mirror putting on my makeup. She used to follow me there, sit herself down right behind me, and watch. When I had finished and went back into the bathroom, she would follow me and wait outside, whether the door was open or closed. It was only in the last few years that she started following me. Charlie and I were her main charges. I miss her so much.

It was a simple burial. David, Charlie, Barney, and I. We sent her off with many pictures of her family, some beautiful bows, and the long socks that I wore yesterday when she died. We also included five mauve-red roses, one from each of us, including Pippin, and a big Christmas bow around her box. Charlie didn't want to leave the site. We had to bribe him away with a biscuit. He lay down with his head pointing in at the edge of the hole, staring at the box that he knew held Sabrina. He barked periodically. I know what he wanted. He wanted Sabrina to get out of the box. Me too, Charlie. No, we have to let her go. It's time, whether we like it or not. We had her for only six and a half years, definitely not enough. I ache.

Sabrina. What a beautiful name. I will forever love her ways, her beautiful face, her intelligence. How lucky I am to have known this one-of-a-kind Sheltie. And this Miss Independent Spirit decided to bond with me. She made me feel so special. Thank you, Sabrina. You too helped to heal my heart. Now I must let you go. Soar, my little girl. That's how I want to remember you. Thank you for stopping by. Your mom loves you.

November 13, 2002

More clean up after the big rain. It's still muddy, so I can't do much gardening. This morning I potted a grass and did some pruning. Even after the rain, I still had to water some.

Sabrina died only a week ago today, but little by little, memories of the happy times with her are coming back. Her bounce, I miss her bounce. Little Button Nose, I would call her. Cute as a button. I can still feel her intense stare. Always staring, because she was always analyzing. Ever so vigilant — I loved that about her.

I miss you, Sabrina. Rest in peace, my brave little munchkin.

November 14, 2002

Some deep watering for the trees along the fence. Jésus had cultivated, cleaned, and dug basins for them on Tuesday, so the time was right.

Went by what used to be R.G. Harris' Nursery in Malibu. Now every single plant, tree, flower, and vine is gone. Then I visited Malibu Garden Center. Looks like Corrine, who was the life force of it, is no longer there. I'm told she's building a barn on the Big Island in Hawaii. It's much quieter at the Center now, just some small chickens and a couple of cats running around, and no ducks. And there are only a few wild grasses. Very different energy now, much more sedate. I miss the aliveness when Corrine was there. I miss R. G. Harris Nursery. Everything changes. And mostly I miss Sabrina.

November 15, 2002

Hot. Winds. And so tomorrow, Saturday, I will be watering a lot. On a break from work, I went to Armstrong's Nursery. Got some dianthus, a miscanthus grass, some petunias, an African daisy, an ivy, and a maidenhair fern. The fern for Sabrina.

Twelve

December 12, 2002

Today is a special day: Barney's designated Birthday! Five years old. Barney — don't you just love the name?

Barney is a magnificent dog: loves people, wants to play, is always but always happy. Pure Golden. Barney is gorgeous: red-gold coat, with a big full tail. And then, to top it off, there are those doe eyes, those eyes that can induce guilt better than any being I know. When he gets that guilt-inducing expression on his face, I call him Mr. Forlorn. Barney makes me smile, makes me laugh. He is so happy. I'm so happy I made the decision to keep him. And I think Charlie is too. The whole family loves Barney, even our sixteen-and-a-half-year-old cat, Pippin. He tolerates Barney giving him sloppy Retriever kisses. A joy, that's what Barney is. Barney Joe Maximilian Lampert. Happy Birthday, Barney! And a million more!

Barney was about eight months old when I rescued him, about four years ago. What a stroke of luck that I was going down the Pacific Coast Highway when Barney was trying to cross it. I remember it so vividly …

I was on my way to work when, out of nowhere, trucks and cars, including mine, began slamming on their brakes, swerving, skidding, smoke coming out of some of them, horns honking. About thirty cars were involved, but amazingly there were no accidents! And ambling his way across the highway, from the beach side, was a dog. How he got through four lanes of traffic on that busy highway, with cars traveling in excess of fifty miles per hour, is still beyond me. Heads were turning, faces had terror on them. But, miraculously, we had all avoided hitting the dog and each other. I looked back at his face as I was leaving the scene. He was looking at all the cars from over his shoulder. The expression on his face seemed to say, "That's incredible, what just happened?"

As I left, I could not get his face out of my mind. He looked like a Golden. I debated whether to go back. It was late. I had a lot of patients to see. Where would I take him? But on instinct, at the next light, I turned around. When I returned to where he was, a woman who seemed frantic was holding him by the collar. He had no tags. I asked her if she knew whose dog it was. No, she didn't. Much to her relief, I said I would take him. I could not leave this dog on the highway — next time he might not be so lucky. He hopped into the back seat of the car. As I glanced in my rearview mirror, he had Leo, my stuffed lion, in his mouth. He looked adorable.

I called David and told him I had a Retriever in the car. David: "Charlie?" Me: "No, another Retriever, I have to get to work." I told David the story of what had happened. It occurred to me that I could bring him to Dr. Olds, go to work, and then David could pick him up at six o'clock that evening. Then we could see about finding his owner. David agreed. The dog was scrawny, wild and young, alert, happy, and smart.

But I did not want to deal with another dog right then. We had lost three of our beloved pets in ten months. Alfie, our sweet Maine Coon cat (Pippin's brother), in September 1997, at age eleven. Mandy, our first Golden, at ten and a half, the following April. And, soon after, Arthur, our Afghan, at ten and a half, in July. When Arthur went, it was more than I could handle. David was as lost and sad as I'd ever seen him. Arthur was his guy. Charlie, when he wasn't digging obsessively in the garden, would be sitting or sleeping next to Sabrina. Also, it was getting close to Charlie's and my birthday. David and I had made plans to go away on a short trip with Sabrina and Charlie. Trying to do some happy things to turn the tide.

When we got to the Brentwood Pet Clinic, I put a leash on the dog, but he was so strong that we still came flying in. The waiting room started spinning, the dog pulling, wanting to say hello to everyone. I heard comments: "Oh, isn't he beautiful," "He's a purebred," "You found him on the highway?" Several of the staff told me, repeatedly, that if we couldn't find the owner, we should keep him. I told them that our house was quiet now, that we had all been through so much, and that the last thing we needed was another dog. It was all happening too fast. At first, I just didn't want this dog to be left on the highway or, worse yet, hit on the highway. Suddenly my life seemed to be getting complicated. I needed time to think.

Well, David picked the dog up at six in the evening and brought him to my office. I could not believe we were involved in this situation. I thought the dog was cute, but not that cute. He had a widow's peak, just like Arthur. I had never seen a widow's peak on a Retriever. And he was similar in color to Mandy, a reddish Golden, looked a lot like her. David and the dog left, and I continued seeing my remaining patients for the day.

On the way home, I put up signs with the dog's description and our phone number. When I got home, there was the question of what to do with him for the night and how to keep him separate from Charlie and Sabrina. Least objectionable solution: he would be fenced in behind the garage, with something to sleep on and some water. It was summer and very pleasant at night.

I called a Golden Retriever rescue group, and they said they had the names of some people who would be very interested, if that was what we wanted to do. One, a retired airline pilot, had an older Golden Retriever and had just lost another, who was twelve years old. He and his wife were at their second home in Mammoth, but they would be back by the end of the week. Another possibility was an accountant and his family in Pacific Palisades. Now we were getting somewhere, I thought.

By the next morning, no one had called to claim the dog. I felt such pressure. I did not want another dog! I was enjoying the quiet of the house and that I could devote my time and energy to other things. For me, the issue now was finding the right home. The best home possible.

The dog spent the night in the back but somehow managed to get out of the area David had so carefully made for him. Amazing. Houdini. Fortunately, the whole back area itself was fenced, so he couldn't run away.

I called the accountant family in the Palisades. It seemed to me they wanted a dog as a toy for their infant child and not for the dog itself. Nope, not good enough. But I was optimistic. The Golden Retriever rescue group had said there would be no problem placing this dog because, as a purebred young Golden, he was highly desirable.

The next day, Wednesday, I had promised my sister that I would go to her gift shop and arrange flowers. David went off to work and, of course, I was left with the dog. So I took him with me. I brought him upstairs to her shop and tied him to a chair. He was really good the whole time I was there! I remember giving him water, holding the dish, and explaining to my sister how I was not taking on the responsibility of one more animal. She just nodded. I was adamant, but I remember she just kept nodding. At that moment, I was sure I wasn't keeping this dog. I couldn't believe that she seemed to not believe me.

No calls that night either. The week went on. Finally, it was too difficult to keep him separated from Charlie and Sabrina, so we let them all be together. The airline pilot and his wife would be back by Friday. They lived in Westlake Village and took their dog on frequent trips to the mountains. Sounded like a good situation for this dog.

Finally, on Friday I spoke with the pilot. But by that point there had been some change in my feelings. I was getting fond of the dog. He was so happy and playful, and he seemed to be getting cuter. So his next home would have to be magnificent. I told the pilot that we would be happy to meet with him and his wife, but we were getting a little attached, and if we let the dog go it would have to be to a great circumstance. The pilot said he understood.

Saturday morning he and his wife showed up. The dog, who by now David had named Barney, went running to the fence to greet them. They seemed to fall in love with Barney and intimated that they would take him right then. They seemed like real dog lovers, so this was a possibility. But I wanted to see their house before we made any decision.

So David, Barney, and I followed them to their home. Nice area and house, but the back yard was a little small — there was no place for an energetic Golden to run. Also, there was a pond in the middle of the back yard. Barney kept going into it, wanting to drink the water. Not clean enough. It was August, and it was blazing hot. We could barely stand to be outside. Barney began looking for something to do. At one point both David and I saw him staring longingly at the edge of the fence, as if to say: "Is that all there is?"

We all went inside. Their older dog didn't want to play. They showed us what would be Barney's dog bed and a couple of toys.

Then they left David and me alone in a room to discuss what we wanted to do. Before they walked out, I started crying just thinking about leaving him. I continued crying. I just couldn't leave him there. I had given myself a test. I had either passed or failed it, depending on how you looked at it. I passed because I couldn't leave him. I failed because I couldn't leave him. And neither could David. We went out to tell them. They were extremely disappointed. Meanwhile, Barney had peed in the living room, which he's never done in any room since, but fortunately that didn't seem to bother them. A little more discussion, a few more tears, and we left, with Barney. I felt bad and good. Bad for the pilot and his wife — I think they hated us — but good that Barney was still with us. And I felt good that we did not leave him there, sweltering and confined in Westlake Village. So it was back to the drawing board.

We told the Golden Retriever rescue group what had happened. They seemed to be getting a little annoyed with us. From their vantage point, they were providing us with perfectly good homes, yet nothing seemed to be good enough for this dog. Well, they came up with another really good possibility. I was excited when I heard about this one. If it wasn't good enough for Barney, maybe I would live there. A 140-acre estate in Montecito! It sounded to me as if this home would be in his best interest. We made contact with the people. She was a flight attendant, and he was a real estate developer. We would meet with them on Saturday. It was now about six days before Charlie's and my birthday. I wanted this situation resolved, so we could enjoy our planned trip to San Ysidro Ranch — also in Montecito — on August 10th with Charlie and Sabrina. A great pre-birthday celebration.

So we arrived in Montecito at this glorious home on top of a hill, but this time without Barney. We were not going to have a repeat of the Westlake situation. We met the woman, but her husband wasn't there. The house was quiet, except for her older, arthritic dog, who had a lot of trouble negotiating the stairs. The front door opened onto a hardwood floor and a railing with about a twenty-foot drop over an indoor swimming pool. A dog like Barney could easily slide through.

She served us tea and told us a bit about herself and her plans for Barney. She had been with the airlines for thirty-one years. She would train Barney in the next ten days, which she had off, and then neuter him. When she was gone, her husband would take care of him. According to her, Barney would be great company for her older dog. Then she showed us around the house. To me, while it was spectacular, with views and glass and of course the indoor pool, the house did not look lived in. Turns out they were renting. She missed her Golden Retriever, who had died a few months ago. He would walk with her to get the mail, which in that house must have been a day's hike.

The house was in an extraordinary setting, and we had a lovely afternoon with her and her dog, but it was not a good enough home for Barney. Her older dog looked in no mood to play. So Barney would be bored. She would be gone for long stretches.

The one hundred forty acres had no fence, so Barney could just wander away. And I could just see him come running into the house excitedly and go flying down into the pool. No, the house was not good enough. We left, and I felt so confused.

As the days went on, I found myself getting more and more attached, and I saw David starting to come to life again. But how could we keep Barney? A Retriever pup requires so much time and attention. And what about Charlie? He was nine. Did he want to deal with a puppy? The days passed. Barney was fitting in. Well, no decision had to be made yet. We would all, including Barney, go to San Ysidro Ranch. We could decide after that. The Retriever rescue group was now clearly annoyed with us. I was getting annoyed with us.

Of course, we all had a great time at San Ysidro. And it was becoming clearer and clearer about Barney. If the Montecito home was not right, then what home would be? David left the decision up to me. On the morning of August 11th, while we were at San Ysidro, I declared that we would keep Barney! Everyone cheered. I felt so relieved. I know David did too. And we never looked back after that morning. It was exactly one week from the day I had found him, but it seemed like a year. It had been such a difficult decision.

With Charlie, Sabrina, and Barney,
the day I decided to keep Barney

Soon after I decided to keep Barney, he ran into me from behind. I sprained my ankle and was on crutches for a week. A week or so after that, he and Charlie got into a huge fight, which I attempted to break up. Almost lost my finger doing that. Charlie bit me, thinking it was Barney. I went to the emergency hospital. Four stitches in my finger — I still have some numbness. Then Barney knocked Sabrina down twice. She twisted her ankle and had to be confined. He's chewed the trim off an old antique wood chest. He's chewed the rug off the bottom stair numerous times. The list goes on. But there has never been a day that I regretted my decision …

Barney is the happiest, most playful dog I have ever known. He idolizes and defers to Charlie, which makes Charlie feel special. Barney's tail wags most of the time — a full, long-haired tail. There's nothing more beautiful than Barney running through the garden, all excited about something, his fur glistening in the sun, his eyes big and bright and happy. Right from the start, what he loved the most was a ball, any ball. He wants to play ball endlessly. First the game was to catch it on one bounce, then on a rebound, then doing whatever he could to make the game harder, sufficiently challenging, because he was so talented and was getting too good for normal games. Four years later, and it's still more of the same. I've lost count of how many balls Barney has — fifty, seventy, a hundred, I just don't know. All I know is that, wherever you look, in the house or in the garden, there are balls, balls of all shapes, balls of all sizes, balls of all colors. He particularly likes balls that make noise and that are soft, light, and rubbery.

Barney loves life, loves and trusts everyone. Before Barney, there was such a stillness in the house. You could cut the grief with a knife. Barney makes everyone smile. Barney has brought love and life and laughter and play back into our home. We all love Barney so much. Never mind that I rescued him — I think he really rescued us. I am so grateful to Barney, and I'm sure everyone else in the house is too.

Are there miracles, and is there magic? I think Barney proves there are both.

Barney

2003

Charlie and me at San Ysidro Ranch

Thirteen

April 15, 2003

Charlie. A quick outpatient surgery. Two days ago, I discovered a lump on the outside edge of his lip. It was black like his lip, so it was hard to see at first. But then it seemed to grow noticeably. Time to contact Dr. Olds.

When I spoke with Dr. Olds, I told him that because of Charlie's age, and because Charlie has not had vaccines in a long time, we didn't want to bring him to the clinic. Graciously, Dr. Olds agreed to see David, Charlie, and Barney at seven last evening at his home. Incredible. What a great man. Compassion and competence, such a rare combination.

After seeing Charlie, Dr. Olds said the thing needed to come off right away. So at nine this morning it was removed, with a local anesthetic. By nine thirty, it was done. Charlie, of course, was his usual, magnificent self. Brave and happy. Pulled through like a champ, again.

Once home, he couldn't get the food in fast enough. The dog is amazing. Thank God I noticed that growth. I can't tell you how much better I felt once it was removed and Charlie was home.

The world seemed right, again.

No Jésus today, even though it was Tuesday. Too much rain the last couple of days. But my garden sparkles after the rain. And Charlie's pulled through yet another surgery, another episode, so I'm happy. I've got him for a little longer.

April 20, 2003

Potted almost everything that was in plastic pots. And of course spent lots of time with my Charlie. Yes, his latest lump was melanoma, but supposedly Dr. Olds got it all, and my comeback kid is doing well: perky, enthusiastic, and his appetite is tremendous. I'm so relieved.

So today was split between Charlie and my garden. My Puppy. I love how he works his way through everything. Charlie, you're the greatest! The love of a dog.

Fourteen

June 23, 2003

I'm looking forward to another trip to San Ysidro Ranch. In a few days, it's David's and my twentieth anniversary. Hardly anyone stays married that long anymore. Twenty years! And we're taking Charlie and Barney too. Should be interesting.

We can't leave Charlie, for many reasons, but primarily we don't want to. Also, who could watch him? He's more than full-time. He needs to go out about every two hours and barks if he's unattended too long. Also barks when *he* thinks it's time to eat. He has to be given his ground barley, sweet potato, and special heart-diet food three times a day. He has hot spots and has to wear an Elizabethan collar if he picks at himself too much. His ears have to be cleaned every two days or so — big wax buildup. He needs someone to sleep with him at night. He needs a million kisses a day. He needs his chest and legs rubbed once or twice a day, and I know there's more. Can't leave Charlie.

And Charlie loves Barney, and Barney loves Charlie. Sooo, Barney has to go too. We'll all head up to San Ysidro Ranch on Wednesday. After our visit, they may change their dog policy.

June 24, 2003

Tuesday, Jésus, good planting day. He planted two westringias near the two big rocks, also some isotoma and nasturtiums along several of the stone paths. I love the orange and yellow colors of the nasturtiums and that they're edible. He also planted a lavender cosmos and some orange roses. When I left for work, Jésus was still planting the roses. Definitely looking good around here. It's turning hot, so I was busy watering. I'm so glad Jésus will be here every day while we're gone, mostly to water.

San Ysidro Ranch is one of my favorite spots on the planet. It's in a natural setting and is a gardener's delight. Its rooms are exquisitely decorated and so comfortable, and the service is excellent. This will be the second time there with Charlie and Barney. Spoiled brats — they don't know the difference. They lead this wonderful, charmed life and just make the assumption that that's the way it's supposed to be, will always be. Good for them. I need some of their attitude.

June 26, 2003

Twenty years ago today, David and I were married, on the beach in Malibu, among family, friends, and my little Cairn Terrier mix, Simon, who wore a big white bow.

Yesterday Charlie, Barney, David, and I piled in the car and drove up here to San Ysidro Ranch, which was no easy feat. Charlie needed the equivalent of a trunk for his things, including his huge round dog bed that's especially good for his joints. The bed is seven inches thick and about five feet across. Also, special food, bandages and wraps, a blanket, sheets, and more. Barney, five and a half, needed only a few tennis balls and a few soft toys. Easy.

We got up here about one in the afternoon and were situated by three thirty in Rose Cottage, which sits on a hill. Lots of rose bushes and trees all around. The cottage has two wood decks, a living room, a bedroom, hardwood floors, old-world comfortable furnishings, and two fireplaces. The look and feel of a bygone era. Of course, neither of the fireplaces can be used, because Charlie needs all the oxygen he can get, and we don't want him breathing smoky air.

At the entrance to Rose Cottage,
San Ysidro Ranch

By the time we arrived, we were all exhausted, even though the ride up was only a little more than an hour. Oh, but the joy of having Charlie and Barney with us on our anniversary is well worth all the effort, including calling the service personnel (four guys) to move the very heavy bed, so that we could pull the rug out more from under it, so that Charlie would have more rug to walk on and less wood floor, which he was having difficulty navigating. That little episode took about an hour and lots of ingenuity. As usual, the service personnel were gracious, accommodating, and understanding about what we needed to do for Charlie.

San Ysidro Ranch prides itself on very high-quality service. As an example of their attitude, a gardener we met yesterday while we were sitting on the lawn waiting for our room to be ready came over this morning with a vase of handpicked roses and wished us a happy anniversary. A purely voluntary act. Later, he would apologize for the vase not being good enough. I love this place. David and I first came to this ranch for our honeymoon, and we have never been disappointed in all the times we have come back.

June 27, 2003

It's morning at San Ysidro, nine o'clock or so. Overcast. A gray squirrel sits on a rooftop. It's quiet. I sit on the deck of our cottage. Last evening, we had a wonderful dinner on the deck, and David gave me a gorgeous platinum bracelet of leaves. All evening we were together with our two Goldens, surrounded by all this beauty. I can't think of a better way to have celebrated our twentieth anniversary.

Charlie's been a real trouper up here. He's adapted so well. I think that, for Charlie, as long as his family is with him, it's okay. And Barney, well, he's having a great time. Maybe the happiest I've ever seen him. He's acting like the mayor of the Ranch, our goodwill ambassador. Friendly? Beyond that. Brings toys and balls to everyone who comes to our cottage. Makes everyone feel good. What a dog *he* is. A real joy. So funny how Barney has become alpha dog here, and yet Charlie seems fine with it. Dogs. They work things out in such subtle ways.

Can I make the time go more slowly? Must promise myself to do this again. That is the only way I will be able to wrench myself out of here.

June 28, 2003

Sun's setting. End of another perfect day. David and I just went for a walk with Charlie and Barney. Sat on the lawn in the middle of the Ranch for a bit. Big wedding party nearby, music playing.

Well, by mistake, a croquet ball came rolling over. Barney, of course, got all excited and put it in his mouth. Some people from the wedding party came over to where we were sitting. Christopher, about two years old, fell in love with Barney — the feeling appeared to be mutual. Kelly, about nine years old, became very concerned about Charlie not having an eye. I had to reassure her. Finally, she sat on the lawn in her pretty white dress, petted Charlie, and noted his smooth fur.

Christopher's parents came over and told us they have to get him a dog, because he loves them so much. So we gave them an oration on Goldens and how great they are, particularly with children. I think we convinced them. We must have spoken with ten other people, mostly about the love of dogs. And, of course, Charlie and Barney were their usual charming selves. Christopher and Kelly were having so much fun their parents had to drag them away, promising they would see the dogs later. What a great exchange of energy.

How can we go home tomorrow? Charlie is having the time of his life: he is alert and raring to go. After walks, he doesn't want to go back into the cottage. I love seeing him so happy. Maybe if we stayed here Charlie *would* live forever. Must come back. Soon.

June 29, 2003

Time to leave. Early morning. Overcast, misty, cool. Quiet. Only the sound of birds singing, and Bach in the further background. My two Goldens are at my feet. In the living room of our wonderful cottage. It's been an oasis here. I feel so much better. For a few days, I was able to hear myself think. The four of us have been inseparable. In the mornings, we all got into bed together, Charlie getting up as far as he could, David helping him the rest of the way. Later we took walks around the Ranch, or read or listened to music, or just rested.

Charlie in Rose Cottage

How quickly the time went. Four days. Poof. I wonder if Charlie and Barney will be as sad to leave as I am. They seem so happy here. Which is amazing for Charlie, because of any being I know, he is the most resistant to change — any kind of change. When he was younger and stronger, it was impossible to get him to budge in most situations if he didn't want to. Like when we'd be on a walk and he'd sit, not wanting to go any farther. Made me laugh. Versus Barney, for whom everything in life is an adventure. Barney seems to love change and new people and new toys and balls and balls and balls and more balls. Barney had a superb time up here. After this, he may find his life in Malibu a little boring.

Another week. That would be good. Would that do it for me? Probably not. A month? Just put my life on hold, patients all wait for me, responsibilities just be quiet for a while. And David and I and Charlie and Barney would continue in the little routine we're all getting used to. But, of course, we can't. I have to just take the wonderful memories home and be happy and grateful for this very special time. A very happy anniversary with our wonderful Goldens, Charlie and Barney, who warm my heart, and make it sing.

Fifteen

July 10, 2003

I've been worried about my Charlie. He had an upset stomach a couple of days ago. And he's a little lethargic today, though tonight he seems a bit better.

I go into such a panic if I think something is wrong with him. These hot summer days are hard on him. I put a cold rag on his head and on the bottom of his feet, then sat with him most of the night. Lots of love. Be lots better tomorrow, Charlie.

July 11, 2003

My Charlie. My Charlie. I found a lump on the side of his neck, just below the place on his lip where I had found the melanoma. Dr. Olds says to watch it. We shouldn't operate, for several reasons. Because Charlie's heart and every other organ probably couldn't take it. And because the tumors they found last year in his liver, adrenals, and the artery to his heart probably have continued to grow, so opening him up might make him worse. In May of 2001,

Dr. Karen Martin had said we were on "bonus time." What are we on now?

July 16, 2003

Sleepless in Malibu. Hot nights. I didn't have to be in to work until later in the day, so I spent a lot of time in the garden, mostly watering. The plants and trees are just soaking up the water. The garden looks lovely. But with all that's bothering me, it's difficult to appreciate it.

And my Charlie, with that stupid lump. I so wish it would go away, but at least it's not getting any bigger. Last night I slept on the sofa, because it was too hot upstairs. Charlie slept on his bed right near me, periodically rolling over to look at me and get some petting. So happy to be petted in the middle of the night. Such a love sponge that dog is. How much longer can I have him?

July 22, 2003

Tuesday with Jésus. It's a hot day. We both worked hard. Jesus planted more myoporum, a couple of podocarpus, and an acacia across from the driveway. It's getting to look gorgeous there. Jésus also planted two flats of baby tears, a blue hibiscus, and a lavatera. Then he took out a Scotch broom, put in a rock rose, and untangled two jasmine plants in pots. We both raked some. I need to go along the fence line and show Jésus the trees and plants that are being covered by the taller trees and should be transplanted. I also need to see what's going on with the citrus trees. They're covered in African daisies and solanum. So much to do. That's good.

My Charlie is having trouble walking. It looks like it's his back again, maybe arthritis. There's so much moisture in the air, which is terrible for arthritic problems. He inches his way along, trying to walk. I can't stand to see him so uncomfortable. What to do? So David and I are doing a lot of research. Maybe an anti-inflammatory supplement like Fresh Factors or Glyco-Flex. The Fresh Factors should help — there are many testimonials about it.

Please let this pass. I'm sitting on Charlie's dog bed with him — he sleeps and snores as I write this. At night, I have a blanket up against his back to keep it warm, which seems to help.

July 24, 2003

Charlie's back is a little better, and there's still no change in the lump. He's happy, but his stomach was upset at lunch two days in a row. Maybe it's the Fresh Factors or the Glyco-Flex. Charlie, if only you could talk. It's so difficult being at work. I want to be with Charlie.

July 25, 2003

Charlie is doing so much better, and that makes me feel so much happier. He still has a little limp and his back seems a bit stiff, but that's a great improvement over how he was on Monday. I'm so grateful. He sleeps very soundly tonight.

Sixteen

August 2, 2003

Well, in ten days it's Charlie's and my birthday. My big guy is going to be fourteen. He sleeps on his dog bed at my feet. Barney sleeps right next to me with his new lavender bear. I'm blessed. Such extraordinary beings. It was a good day.

August 9, 2003

Saturday. David threw a wonderful early birthday party for me, with some very special friends. Among them was my cousin Myrna, who's been so supportive of me and has a deep abiding love for animals. Also there was my very good friend Paul, whom I've known for thirty years and who teaches at UCLA and elsewhere.

There were balloons, cake from the Ivy, and Cornish hens with David's orange sauce. Mmmmm. Great cheeses, salad and a variety of ice creams. For presents, I was given plants, of course — rose bushes, a veronica bush, and more. It was a warm, cozy night. We spent the time mostly sitting in the garden, talking and laughing.

Charlie insisted on coming out and sitting with everyone. I think he was mostly interested in the cheese. I couldn't get him back in the house. When I would ask him to come in, he would throw his paw in the air. Everyone laughed — they thought that was cute. It was.

August 10, 2003

Sunday was cleanup, watering and gardening, and then a movie, *Pirates of the Caribbean*. Fun. Love Johnny Depp.

Hot August days and nights. I hope the vegetation survives all this heat. Charlie was born in the middle of this heat. Me too.

August 11, 2003

I wish I could turn back the hands of time. I'm thrilled that Charlie has made it to fourteen, but I wish we both could be younger, go back to when Charlie was a puppy living with Mandy and Arthur ...

Mandy was alpha dog then. Charlie used to love playing with her, wrestling and tugging at toys. Two energetic Goldens, they seemed to understand each other. Charlie would follow Mandy around the yard while she made her rounds, nose to the ground, looking for who knows what. He would watch her intently as she dug hole after hole, which she loved to do. Then he would start a hole of his own, and she would oversee his work. You could see that he loved being with her and learning from her.

With Arthur and Charlie, it was very different — two intact males who had to learn how to live together. Most of the time, Charlie was respectful of Arthur, and Arthur was very patient with him. And I think Charlie was intrigued by this beautiful Afghan with his long flowing hair. But they could also be very funny together. For example, somehow they decided that Arthur was in charge of protecting the outside of the house and Charlie was in charge of protecting the inside. When someone would come to our front door, it would be Charlie who would greet and evaluate them, while Arthur held back. When someone would walk by our property, it would be Arthur who would run out to the fence line to bark at them. Although occasionally Charlie would forget the rules and run out and start barking right next to Arthur. If that happened, Arthur would get annoyed at Charlie and start barking at *him*, forgetting about the passerby, who generally would have left long before Charlie would get the message to stop barking and go back into the house.

Mandy and Arthur gave Charlie a wonderful puppyhood …

David and I spent today in Summerland and Montecito. We were planning to go to another movie tonight, but when we came home Charlie didn't seem right. So plans had to change: we needed to be with Charlie. We opened some doors and windows, and once he got a few hours of air, he seemed a lot better.

So then we could go out for a little while. First a "garden tour" in Malibu, mostly on Point Dume. We came to a house that looked like a castle. There was a gentle young Golden Retriever in the front behind a gate. We petted him through the bars. Terrible watchdogs. Some women passing by asked curtly if we knew the woman who lives there. I said we didn't. One said that the woman is extremely sick. I suppose it was a way of telling us to leave. So we said goodbye to the Golden and left.

For me, there was a big lesson in what had just happened. That house was impressive, with gorgeous plantings, and was probably worth ten million dollars or more. Everything was perfect, down to the Golden Retriever, but inside was a very sad story. There probably wasn't much play in that house, and I know how much Goldens like to play. So I got shocked into appreciating my life and not longing for something different and more.

From there we went to Geoffrey's restaurant on the Malibu coast, with a glorious view of the ocean, the moonlight full upon it. A magical scene. We had salads, wine and dessert. It was fun and light, and I'm happier. Came home to Charlie doing fine: he had just needed some air before. That heart and those lungs needed air.

August 12, 2003

Happy Birthday to Charlie and me. There were cards and lots of singing and laughing this morning, with Charlie on his back, throwing his paws in the air. I'm so happy I have Charlie on this birthday. David took some cute pictures of Charlie and me, David getting impatient with the two of us, Charlie and I getting impatient with David and the picture-taking. I'm not even thinking about my age. I feel the same as I felt last week. I'll just keep plowing ahead, making my life meaningful and rich, thankful for what I have. And giving Charlie as much love as possible.

Charlie and me on our birthday, in the garden
(Charlie turns fourteen)

Seventeen

August 25, 2003

My dear Charlie. The lump in his neck looks bigger. Dr. Olds tomorrow, at least to talk to. We've got to know the options. Charlie, please give us more time together.

August 26, 2003

Saw Dr. Olds last night, again at his house. He was kind and compassionate. Charlie's lump is getting bigger. Damn. Appears it's in his lymph node, and it's probably malignant. We might have to take it out. But if we operate, what about his heart? Could it withstand the operation? What about all the things wrong with him? We've got a horrible decision to make. I feel awful. How many surgeries and problems can one dog have? Dr. Olds was surprised to see how well Charlie was walking. Little trouper. I wish that lump would just disappear.

I gardened some today but was so sad. My mind kept drifting to Charlie.

September 1, 2003

Still working on the tough decision regarding Charlie. The lump in his neck is getting even bigger. So do we operate and take a big chance? Or look for something less invasive? Is there anything less invasive? Do we take him to different doctors to get other opinions? What do we do with this magnificent dog? His life is dependent on us. I can hardly stop thinking about it and I can barely stand thinking about it.

Dear Charlie, what do you want? Oh, I know. You want to live forever with me and David and Barney and Pippin and any dog we decide to bring into the house. Oh how I wish you could. I wish you didn't have to have so many things wrong with you. Your will — your will is the strongest, by far, of any part of you. I love your incredibly strong will. My big alpha dog. So determined.

Puppy, I've got a hard decision to make, but I will figure out what to do. You can count on me, as I can count on you. Thank you again for being there for me and showering me with love. You probably have little idea what you've done for me. I love you, Charlie.

September 2, 2003

So it looks like we're scheduling surgery for Charlie. There's no really good choice. The lump is not going away, it's not staying the same size, it's not getting better or looking or feeling innocuous. I'm sick inside. I love this dog so much. I'm sitting with Charlie, on a rug on the kitchen floor, while he sleeps. Periodically he raises his paw, looks at me, and wants me to pet him. My Charlie. Please let him pull through this surgery. Please give us more time.

It's hard to do any writing. He keeps turning and looking at me. What's the right thing to do? This morning, Dr. Olds said there is no right choice. What does Charlie want? He wants to be here. He wants us to try. I don't get the sense that he's done. He still looks forward to his walks, his food, and his family. Moving slowly, but moving. So we all must continue to fight on.

September 3, 2003

I can barely concentrate on anything. Charlie is going to have yet another surgery. The lump. I'm sick. I woke up in the middle of the night and couldn't sleep, so I got into bed with Charlie. He looked at me in disbelief. He was so happy that he rolled onto his back, legs straight in the air. Finally, we settled into spooning: I petted him, and whenever I stopped, he would roll over and throw a paw in the air. This went on for about an hour until we both fell asleep. The sweetness of that dog. I pray he pulls through this surgery. This awful melanoma is aggressive. First his conjunctiva, then his eye, then his mouth and now, it appears, a lymph node. Please dear God make it be okay for this big gentle soul.

Charlie was really bright and alert today. David thinks it's because I slept next to him. Oh Charlie. Be tough, my guy. Get through this and let's have some more good times together. I'll keep at this as long as you want, dear Charlie. Forever would be fine with me.

September 4, 2003

My mind drifts to Charlie no matter what I do. Five days from today is his surgery. I know he wants to stay around as long as possible. I want that too.

I slept near him again last night. He was on his dog bed, and I was on the sofa right above him. I can't tell you how many times he turned to me to be petted. And then, with the first hint of the morning light, it was nonstop.

September 5, 2003

This morning, Charlie went to see Dr. Karen Martin in Thousand Oaks for blood work and a chest X-ray. She's an extremely smart veterinarian. Totally focused on the animals.

David and Barney took Charlie. I had to work. Well, I got a full report. Last time she saw Charlie was two and a half years ago. That was when she said we were on "bonus time." This morning she was quite impressed. She said he looked really good, and she could tell he was getting great care. I hear Charlie was his old incredible self: solid, poised, calm, alert, and interested in Gwen, a female Border Collie. Wish I could have been there to see that.

According to Dr. Martin, Charlie has a slight heart murmur but otherwise looks to be in good shape. We need to see the blood test results before we definitely say yes to surgery. David tells me that everyone at the clinic fell in love with both Charlie and Barney. Barney's no slouch, either.

So four days from now Charlie may or may not have surgery. Oh what's the best thing to do? By Tuesday we'll have figured it out, I'm sure. Results from his blood work should help.

Keep fighting, Charlie. I know you still love your life.

September 6, 2003

Saturday. It's hot, so there's lots of watering. Sticking close to home, to be with Charlie.

Please be okay, Charlie. Give us more time together, please. Please, Dr. Olds, get all the melanoma. And dear, sweet Charlie, please stop growing things.

Saw my friend Pat today. She's in her eighties, paints in oils, and is a master gardener. Lives on a nearby hill with a sweeping view of the ocean. We got our beautiful Afghan, Arthur, from her. She called yesterday and said she had a book she thought I might like: *So Long, See You Tomorrow* by William Maxwell. I love what she said about Charlie and me — that we "live in a circle together." That sounds so true. Right now, in fact, we are both on his big round dog bed, touching. I can feel his pure, solid energy.

I went to the Malibu Garden Center and bought just a few plants. But mostly I spent the day with Charlie. We sat outside on the lawn with Barney for a bit. Charlie loved that. Me too. I ache inside. I'm trying to not let it show and trying to not give in to it. I want to be strong and cheerful for Charlie. I want him to feel love and joy all around him. Yes, Charlie and I live in a little circle. I love thinking about us that way.

September 7, 2003

I did lots of watering and potted some new plants, but that was about it. I didn't have much enthusiasm for the garden; I'm far too upset about Charlie.

My tired boy wasn't very happy today, has an upset stomach. Maybe tomorrow will be a better day, and then supposedly the day after that he will have surgery. We've got to get the blood work back first.

Charlie, dear sweet Charlie, what do you want? To be young again. To be with Mandy and Arthur. To run around in the garden. To bark at one thing or another. To have a bounce in your step.

Charlie, I wish you could have all that again. I wish you and I could start all over and relive every moment. It looks like we can't and we have to wind down. But I'll be with you all the way. Don't worry. I love you so much, Charlie. Such a loyal, good pal. I love that you still care where I am, still get happy to see me. You warm my heart. I can't say it enough. I love you, Charlie.

September 8, 2003

Monday. Charlie's blood work came back okay. So it looks like he will have surgery tomorrow. I'm so scared. Please be okay Charlie. Charlie, I'm doing what I think is best for you. It looks like we can't leave that growth in there. We have to get it out. The surgery is scheduled for early in the morning. Please let it be smooth, with no glitches and very little pain.

I was with Charlie most of the day, didn't want to be too far away. I did some errands in the morning, then came back like a homing pigeon. Also, I canceled all my appointments for today and tomorrow.

Charlie's resting on his bed at my feet. I had sat on the couch, and he had been across the room, but then he got up and walked over to be near me. Now it's not that easy for Charlie to get up these days. Joints, stomach. The trouper. Through all this he is still working on our connection. I can feel it. I feel the bond. I brushed him, cleaned his ears, towel washed him. Barney too. They look and smell great. Could we just skip to tomorrow night and have everything be fine? Dr. Olds, could you get it all? And could it be contained? And could Charlie get another fourteen years, please?

Charlie went for a few walks today and did pretty well. I've got to make sure that that heart is in good shape for tomorrow. I'm told that the anesthesia is state-of-the-art, but I wish there were some way to do this without putting him under. I just want to see his smiling face at the end of the operation. That face.

Dr. Olds says that when Charlie wakes up he can go home. He sleeps soundly now and looks so peaceful.

September 9, 2003

Flying colors! Charlie made it through his surgery! I'm so happy. He marched into the operating room at about nine in the morning and was out by noon. Dr. Olds, Charlie's wonderful surgeon and vet, got all of the growth that he could. Yes, it was a malignant melanoma. In his lymph node. Probably some cells in the other nodes. A branch of his jugular vein was nicked to remove the part of the melanoma that was growing around it. Thus, Charlie has to wear a bandage around his head for twenty-four hours. A babushka, we're calling it. He looks adorable.

David stayed with Charlie throughout the entire surgery. I just couldn't do that, so I sat with Barney in the car. Charlie's Aunt Myrna dropped by to lend support. I was more than worried that Charlie wouldn't make it through the surgery, and I was so relieved to hear that it was over and he was waking up. I went in for a minute while he was in recovery. He turned his head, looked me in the eye, and lifted his paw, even though the anesthesia still hadn't worn off. Incredible dog. Oh I'm so relieved. We have more time. But I know that it may be very limited.

David tells me that everyone at the clinic was really good to Charlie, gentle and kind. My big guy. Big Golden. Fourteen. That's big, Charlie. Charlie, I'm so proud of you, of your intent, serious, focused spirit, and how you forge ahead through any and all of life's obstacles. I love you so much. And I love how our connection matters so much to you. Me too, Charlie. You were magnificent today. You came through almost an hour of surgery — even with your heart murmur! I'm more than proud. Charlie, you know I'll do whatever it takes.

We're looking into a clinical trial for you. It's the newest treatment for the melanoma. It involves nine shots of a vaccine over a nine-week period, and supposedly there are no side effects. And Charlie, I will be with you as much as is humanly possible. I know how much that means to you. Me too, Charlie. I love you, my old soul. You're my treasure. Sleep, my big guy.

Eighteen

September 10, 2003

Charlie is incredible. Fourteen years old and so many things wrong, yesterday surgery, and yet today alert, voraciously hungry, and happy-looking. The babushka came off today, so I can see that puppy face again. Each day is precious.

Managed to do some gardening today, mostly watering. Tomorrow Jésus — on Thursday this week, because Tuesday was for Charlie. The plan is to clean some grasses near the green bench, maybe to plant some jasmine, but mostly to cultivate and dig basins. I so appreciate that garden. Even though lately my heart has not been in it, the fact that it begs to be watered every day is good for me — it forces me to concentrate on something else besides my sadness about Charlie.

September 11, 2003

September 11th. Two years. A Thursday. Jésus spent four hours pruning, trimming, and cleaning the pampas grasses — he did an excellent job. They look gorgeous with their new plumes. While many plants and flowers are getting ready for the winter and have had their growth spurt, the pampas are in all their glory now. I've always loved them: they always look good.

I did a lot of the cleaning up and pruning myself. It was so good to spend time in the garden. It helped me.

My Charlie continues to improve. His appetite is good, and he looks alert. Next week we start him on the vaccine to try to eradicate any remaining cancer cells. It may mean more time for my Charlie.

September 12, 2003

Sad. Oh, I know Charlie pulled through his surgery really well, but his appetite is inconsistent, and his stomach is upset. I just tell myself I have to give Charlie really good days. Every day has to be good for him.

Last night, about three in the morning, he began to bark. There he was, sitting straight up, looking pretty alert. We let him out, but when he came back in, he was quite sluggish. That scared me, so I slept on the sofa right above him. After a while, he turned to me and wanted to be petted, again and again and again, until finally we both fell asleep.

Almost the weekend, thankfully, then I can be with him a lot more. I'm looking forward to that so much. Maybe we'll watch movies and I'll spend time in the garden, watering, repotting, adding new soil and some fertilizer to the plants in pots.

Sometimes I can be really rational about Charlie, but most of the time I can't.

September 13, 2003

Happy today, so I spent a lot of time in the garden. Charlie is doing so much better. His stomach seems to be settling, and he seems to have some energy. He's far more alert, and is getting up on his own. And his appetite's good. On his walk tonight he got down on his haunches and went nose-to-nose barking and growling at a neighbor's dog at the bottom of their wood fence. I loved seeing him be so aggressive. Charlie's still doing his job.

In the garden I did some raking — there are lots of leaves all over. Also did a little arranging. Overcast most of the day. Fall just around the corner. Now that the summer's endless heat wave appears to be passing, maybe I can focus on something besides watering. I still need to transplant the peach tree that's in almost total shade, also to plant the jasmines, cultivate, and plant some of the many potted plants.

I brought some chocolate chip cookies to Dr. Olds. For his love and care of Charlie, for his dedication and competence, for his kindness, and for his staff, who have been so good to us. I could tell he was touched. What a gracious man. He's the best. I hope he never retires.

Charlie will get his stitches out in another week, and then next Friday he'll start his nine-shot vaccine regimen, which hopefully will fight the melanoma. Thirty percent chance, they say. I'll take it.

I know our time is limited. But today Charlie looked so perky, and I know he felt better. It was a great day.

September 14, 2003

A Sunday, still overcast.

Charlie continues to improve, although tonight on his walk he got fatigued. He walked home slowly and looked a little out of it. However, when he heard other dogs barking he got that aggressive look on his face: ears forward, head looking big.

When we got home he flopped on his bed and went to sleep. I sat with him and stroked him. And then, within a half hour, he was rolling on his back, feet in the air. What can I say about this dog? Indomitable spirit.

Not much gardening today. Some watering — there's always that to do. Tomorrow I have so many errands that even if I started at two in the morning, I don't think I would finish. But it's cooler, and I am not so tethered to the garden. So I can think about getting other things done.

I've got Pippin up here in the bedroom. He sits proudly on

the bed, cleaning himself periodically. What a great cat: seventeen years old, gorgeous, so well adjusted, cool, and calm. But even he can't break my dog fixation. Dogs, just the sight of one makes me happy. I even like sitting at clinics watching the dogs with their owners.

Now I need to go to sleep so that I can have a full day. Have to get through all those errands, so I can spend time with my Charlie. His name. I just love his name.

September 15, 2003

A Monday. Off for the day. Lots of time with Charlie. He's doing well, but I see the subtle changes. His legs aren't very strong; they give out on him. So he walks very carefully, compensating. I think it's heart-related. But I love how hard he tries — he just keeps pushing through. We even went for a few walks today. He still loves his walks.

This afternoon I lay with him for a while. We cuddled. He kept rolling on his back and putting his paws in the air. So cute. At night I brought him outside, so he could breathe some fresh air before going to sleep. He seemed to love that, sitting on his bed, taking in the night air. Oh, could this go on endlessly? That would be fine. Twice today he came looking for me in the house. He walked in wagging his tail, with that smile on his face, and I melted, again. That dog. That one of a kind. My Charlie.

September 17, 2003

Fall. Yesterday Jésus cleaned the rest of the grasses. They look great. And he transplanted the peach tree. It had started out in the sun but got covered by a ficus that became huge. Also, he cleaned out some African daisies that also had gotten too shaded.

Suzie, who owns the neighborhood cleaners, called today and said she had some flowering ginger for me. David picked them up — three big roots. I put them in some soil in a terra cotta pot, and next Tuesday Jésus can plant them. How nice of her to think of me. I hope they take. Supposedly the ginger flower smells fantastic.

Did some watering today, but that was about it. I had to get in to work early. For the next few weeks, my focus in the garden will be to clean up, prune, cultivate, and dig basins. Must resist getting new plants.

Charlie, he has his good days and his bad days. Today he seemed pretty happy, and he ate well. But yesterday, according to David, his appetite was not so great. When I came home last night, Charlie wanted to be with me, so he came up the stairs into the kitchen. We sat on the rug in there for a while. I read, he slept. I petted him, he looked at me if I stopped. Everyone keep their fingers crossed for Charlie.

Nineteen

September 19, 2003

This afternoon Charlie went to the oncology clinic for the vaccine. Dr. Sabhlock met with us. We all sat in the hallway, because the consulting room was too hot and there was not enough air flow for Charlie. Barney was there, of course. As we walked in, there were a number of dogs and owners in the waiting room. All of them, like us, hoping against hope. It's serious when you get to this clinic. A number of the dogs had sad faces, shaved areas, lines drawn on their bodies. And then there were a few whose tails wagged. All I know is that I could never work there.

The doctor and all the staff were women in their twenties and thirties. When Dr. Sabhlock walked over to us, Charlie got up to greet her. Barney of course was all over her, trying to give her kisses. She sat on the floor, Charlie sat in my lap, Barney could not keep still, and David sat leaning against the wall. She wanted Charlie's history. She had his chest X-rays and his blood work. We told her about the melanoma first appearing in his conjunctiva three years ago, then in his eye that was removed two years ago, then this year on his lip and, most recently, in his lymph node.

She was more than incredulous that the melanoma had been around for such a long time and that Charlie had survived it all. She even referred to him as a "miracle dog." How did she make that assessment so quickly? We told her about his starting to go into a coma a year ago, the vigil, and the Tahitian noni juice. And how after about five days he started to pull out of it. She was astonished.

Later we talked about statistics for the vaccine she was about to administer to Charlie. David noted that in the literature, dogs with Charlie's condition are given only a thirty percent chance. She said, "This dog, I'd give a fifty percent chance."

Charlie sat up through the whole half-hour discussion. He seemed to be listening. I kept petting him. At one point, she spoke of giving him an MRI to look at his stomach. I said that my philosophy at this point was to give Charlie the best quality of life possible, nothing invasive or uncomfortable, and nothing risky. So I think she and I understood one another.

Charlie was his extraordinary self today. He made it just fine through the long ride to Sherman Oaks and from the car to the clinic. It must have been ninety degrees there. I put cold wet paper towels on his head as soon as we arrived.

He sat patiently while we all talked about his fate, and he didn't flinch with the shot — my stoic, strong dog. I know he felt good having his family around him. For the next twenty-four hours, we have to watch him closely to make sure he doesn't have an adverse reaction to the vaccine. Charlie is now being given the most advanced treatment there is for melanoma.

When it was time to leave, he just about pranced to the door; he definitely wanted to go. That place was a bit drab — gray carpet, white walls, long empty halls — and oh the sickness that inhabits those rooms. I heard that one dog comes from Lake Havasu. Actually, I love hearing that people are so devoted to their pets.

The doctor had been nice and seemed to genuinely like animals. She had even played with Barney a bit, which made Barney happy. Before we left, I put alcohol on the pads of Charlie's feet and more wet paper towels on his face to cool him off. David drove us home, the two dogs with me in the back, lots of air conditioning. I had Charlie's head in my lap, and Barney leaned on me and at times on Charlie.

I'm so proud of Charlie and the way he conducts himself. He's dignified, and he accepts what needs to be done. He trusts David and me. He's on his bed now, resting from his big day. I hope this vaccine does some good. My magnificent dog. He showed that again today. Maybe we bought some more time. I hope. I hope.

Twenty

September 21, 2003

Sunday. When I wasn't with Charlie, I was in the garden. Charlie is managing. His stomach seems better, and his appetite is good, but now he's having a lot of trouble walking and getting up from a lying or sitting position. It pains me to see him like this. Though we did walk three times today. He walks gingerly and concentrates, just keeps pushing ahead. Bless him. That will is going to outlive everything.

Lots of watering today, but it is cooling down, and I'm glad that the summer has passed. I think it was two months of nonstop heat. I got rid of some plants that were not doing well — daylilies, alyssum, and more. That felt good. I'm really trying to clean and organize what's here, so I'm restraining myself from buying new plants. Tuesday, when Jésus comes, I want him to plant some potted jasmines and cultivate and dig basins along the eastern fence.

Now it's time for sleep. I'm off tomorrow, so I'll probably garden more. That helps so much. Sleep well, Charlie.

September 22, 2003

Monday. Charlie struggles. It's his stomach. He saw Dr. Olds today and had his stitches out. His heart's good, only a slight murmur, but walking is still difficult. He's wobbly, shaky, and not able to get up much on his own. He falls. His appetite is erratic: he'll eat some but then stops. Tomorrow lamb chops. I hope he likes them.

I'm sick inside. How much more time do we have?

I'm sleeping on the sofa right above his bed. Will that help? What can I do? His legs are moving. Are you dreaming, Charlie? Are you running in your dream? He lifts his paw some when he wants me to keep petting him. He looks me in the eye. He still cares when I come and go. Started to roll on his back slightly tonight. Please don't be in any pain, Charlie. I don't think you are too uncomfortable. I will watch you closely.

Slowing down. Though he did stop by that same spot at the fence today, probably in hope of fighting with a dog. That very strong will. Will it outlive him? Tough guy. I rub his legs and back ten, twenty times a day. I wish I could bring them back to life. I don't want him to force himself to be okay. Don't do that for me, Charlie. Be how you feel. He just rolled all the way over on his back, feet in the air. I love seeing that. That's a good sign. I'm looking for any good signs. Fourteen years. Where did they go? Good night, my Charlie.

CHARLIE

September 24, 2003

Appetite poor. Does not want to eat. Periodically drinks water.
I'm so sad. Is this it? Going to give him aloe juice and Green
Magma. All to try to neutralize his stomach. Terrible sour acidic
stomach. He rests on the kitchen floor. Have tried chicken livers,
Artemis canned food, Nutri-Cal, water with liver flavoring — he
won't eat anything. I rubbed the Nutri-Cal on his teeth. I bathed
him with a hand towel. I love him so much. It aches in my throat.
Called the Pets Naturally store and a homeopathic doctor. David
is at the Vitamin Barn getting the aloe juice and Green Magma.
What will bring Charlie back? Charlie, do you want to come
back?

September 25, 2003

It's a whole new day. That dog. Well, today he ate. Over the
last couple of days we've tried liver, lamb chops, hamburger, eggs,
and more. Today he ate Barney's kibble. Go figure. What is going
on with him? This morning he went to Dr. Lisa's office in Malibu
for a blood panel and urinalysis. We'll have the results tomorrow
morning. He's walking a bit better. He did eat biscuits, both last
night and this morning. Thinking that would be all he would eat, I
bought him a bunch of really healthy ones. I also got a lot of them
from the market last night. He devoured them. Biscuits. That little

brat. Holding out for biscuits.

This morning he seemed so much better. Rolled on his back. But even at one point yesterday, in the throes of being miserable, he backed up into my lap and sat down, the way he's done since he was a puppy. Fighter. Little fighter. Maybe the blood work and urinalysis will reveal something.

And then there's the question of the vaccine tomorrow. What to do? Did the vaccine cause any of this? Or is it the melanoma, his heart, or something else? You'd think that with all the vet visits, he wouldn't want to go near the car. No. This morning, after he came home from Dr. Lisa's and we took him out for a walk, he stood by the car, indicating that he wanted to get in again. My Charlie. My big guy. The spirit, the energy that lives inside of him. I know he's one of a kind.

September 26, 2003

End of a very long day. Ten thirty at night. It's Charlie. Crisis with his liver, a bladder infection, labored breathing. The vet, Dr. Lisa, came to our house. David's giving Charlie subcutaneous fluids, with ampicillin. I had to go to work this morning — had to — for three hours. Wrenched myself out of here — it was so hard to leave. Charlie was in terrible shape this morning. Won't eat. What does this all mean anyway? He couldn't have his melanoma vaccine this week.

Oh my God, how much does this dog have to go through? He's fighting. He wants to live, I can tell. At one point he got annoyed that I was scratching Barney, nudged me with his head. Now mind you, he cannot walk. But still that strong, aggressive, fighting spirit, through all of this. How much more can he withstand? How much more will he fight, with this spirit that I adore? I love how strong and determined and downright annoyed he gets. Bless you, my big guy. I'll fight as long as you want.

September 29, 2003

Charlie died. The last few days have been a blur. He died in my arms, in the garden. David and I were hugging and kissing him and telling him how much we love him. Dr. Lisa was on the phone guiding us as Charlie was taking his last breaths. She said to tell him that it is okay to go. I did. I told him that earlier in the day. He seemed to be pleading with me. I love Charlie so much. It was torture watching him these last few days. Yes, there were moments when he rallied, but mostly he was going downhill. There's a part of me that is relieved because he does not have to struggle anymore, and there's a part of me that would give anything to spend just one more minute with him.

Oh my God how he fought. Three years with melanoma — it's unheard of. I swear these last few weeks and maybe even longer it was just his will that kept him going. Almost all his organs were in trouble, particularly his liver. In Chinese medicine, the liver is the seat of emotions. Doesn't that just fit for Charlie?

Oh my beloved Charlie, did I give you everything you wanted? Were you the happiest dog? My strong-willed, determined guy. There is no dog like Charlie. There will never be a dog like Charlie.

Oh, it was just a week ago he had his stitches out. He walked up and down the road by our house. But then, in the middle of the week, he started not feeling good. His appetite was up and down, and the blood work showed elevated liver and kidney levels, and there was more. Oh yes, and a severe bladder infection. So much wrong. When he wouldn't eat during the week, I looked for the tastiest biscuits I could find. But then his breath got very bad. My friend Pat suggested baking soda in the water, which was a good idea. I called Andrena, of Pets Naturally, who had recommended the noni juice last year when Charlie was heading into a coma and who had recently suggested the aloe juice to try to neutralize his acidity. A pet sitter I interviewed on Wednesday, who saw what was going on, suggested the Green Magma powder. By Thursday, all this seemed to get his acid stomach under control.

Friday, I found myself waking up at four in the morning and getting in bed with Charlie. I could tell he loved that. And I did too. David had already given him subcutaneous fluids and was sleeping on the sofa near Charlie.

I had to go to work that morning, not knowing if I would ever see Charlie again. He was doing so poorly. Not eating. Not drinking much. I was so sick at heart, with an awful ache in my throat. I worried that he would go into some painful situation.

When Dr. Lisa came over that afternoon, she seemed to have some hope. But I think she was trying to be optimistic, because we were trying to be optimistic, and because the day before, Charlie had eaten a biscuit at her office. He tried with all his might. Sheer determination and tenacity.

Saturday I had to go in to work for a few hours, but I got home as quickly as possible. I even rented three movies, thinking maybe we'd have a cozy weekend and Charlie would feel better. It's hard to think that by Saturday he only had one more day to live.

Saturday night was awful. He could not get comfortable. Temperature of 104 degrees. Shortly before midnight, we took him outside and laid him on the lawn. Nice and cool. Earlier, I had called vets, pet stores, and emergency hospitals, to see what to do about the temperature. Alcohol on the pads of his feet. Cool towels on his neck and under his arms. It all worked. His temperature came down. Eventually, it was normal.

But by Sunday he looked weak to me. Out on the lawn again, and I sat with him. I rubbed him and scratched him, and ever so slightly he lifted his paw. It was so beautiful to see. Selfishly, I had wanted him to do that one last time. I knew he would never be able to do that again.

Dr. Lisa came over on Sunday too, and Charlie even stood up briefly and relieved himself while she was here. We were all so proud. We got a little encouraged, though I think I was far more skeptical than David and the doctor. Because I know my Charlie. He would do whatever he had to do to rise to the occasion, but that didn't mean everything was okay.

Saturday night I had started getting sick, couldn't breathe out of the right side of my nose, sore throat, tired, and headache. Came out of nowhere, which is so unusual — I always have some warning. And then Sunday I was really sick. I was so mad. I wanted to be there one hundred percent for Charlie. So mostly I just tried to ignore how sick I was.

I held Charlie, scratched him, kissed him, talked in his ear. Charlie I love you. Charlie you are the best dog. Charlie you have made me happier than any being. Charlie what do you want now? Do what you want. You will always be my Puppy. I will always be your mom. If there's a place to meet later we will. I don't know how much of this he understood, but it was important for me to tell him everything that day. I knew there wasn't much time.

It was early Sunday evening. I was lying on the couch right above Charlie. Periodically, he would get comfortable. But for the most part he wasn't. I was holding his head, looking at his face, stroking him.

In the midst of all this, at night now, Barney came running into the house with a dead rabbit in his mouth. He'd never done that before. David dealt with it.

When Charlie relieved himself, I could tell it was a strain for him. Too much. We called Dr. Lisa. And then the room started spinning. David held Charlie up, thinking that might help him breathe. But it was more than that. Charlie was dying. Oh my God. We took him outside on the lawn, held him, and stroked him.

He fought to the very end. He put up such a good fight.

Charlie, I am proud of you. So very proud of you. I think you always knew that. I treasure you, Charlie. I will always and forever miss you. May you rest in eternal peace, you very good soul you. How pure you are. Oh how I will miss your purity. Please my big guy, know that I love you with all my heart and that you have made me so happy, so very happy.

Oh my God, what if I had never wanted to take that big puppy out of the glass case in the pet store for some exercise? Fourteen years with Charlie I would have missed, fourteen years of bliss. A fluke, a chance meeting, and look who I got. Charlie. Wherever you are, be well. I'm so happy we crossed paths. I love you my Puppy.

Twenty-One

September 30, 2003

Tuesday. So very sad. My sidekick.

Last night I said goodbye to my Charlie. David, Barney, and I. Yellow flowers for a Golden, pictures of all his family, cards and letters from each of us, some of my clothing from the day before — the top I wore, my socks.

I sang our song to him. "You make me feel so young ... running across the meadow, picking up all those forget-me-nots." Later played it over and over, for hours. Our happy song.

I ache. How will I work my way through this? Everywhere I look, in the house and in the garden, reminds me of Charlie. Maybe writing will help. Please something help.

Almost, this is too much for me. A piece of me feels missing, that I'll have to learn to live without. Charlie gave me energy and confidence and courage. Charlie always made everything better. But Charlie can't make this better.

I miss Charlie. I miss Charlie. I miss Charlie. Please can I have Charlie back, for a few minutes? For a minute? Charlie, I wish I could kiss you just one more time.

Charlie, I hope you know all that you mean to me. Rest in peace, my beautiful boy.

October 2, 2003

Afternoon. In a bit of a fog. Have to concentrate very hard at work. It's so difficult. Last night when I got home from work, there at the door were Jan's Wow Bow Biscuits from New York. I ordered them last week and asked that the order be rushed. Charlie loved these biscuits. I can see why. They look and smell delicious. Made me sad to see them, knowing how much Charlie loved them.

Everything seems to make me sad. Watering this morning made me sad. Taking Barney for a walk made me sad. Folding my clean clothes made me sad. Sad, sad, sad. On the verge of tears all day. Human contact helps some.

I went to a nursery, got some plants. It was easier right after Charlie died. It's more difficult now. How could Charlie die? How can he not be here anymore? How can I just live with memories and pictures? Please come back somehow, Charlie.

October 3, 2003

Got through my work week without Charlie. I miss him so much, feel like I'm operating with only half of me. Will this heavy fog lift? I think about him constantly and obsessively.

I wonder what his pal Barney is thinking and feeling. He must miss him. What does Barney understand about what happened? I'm giving Barney lots of love, for him and for me. Kissing him a lot. I miss kissing Charlie. I miss kissing him in his ear. When he started getting hard of hearing, I would talk into his ear, as if it were a megaphone. I loved seeing him get happy over something I said. What could it have been like for him to lose a lot of his hearing? Well, we managed — lots of hand signs and clapping. Through it all, we kept our connection up, both worked hard at it. It was important to both of us.

I ache in my throat, tears welling up. Terrible feeling. I'm overwhelmingly sad. I've got to get through it, got to. I would do better if I knew I were going to see him again. Pet his beautiful, blond fur. Gorgeous, handsome dog. Big. Big head. Big body. I loved how big he was. Like being with another person, only better.

Charlie. Fourteen years were not enough. I want more. Part of me is irrationally angry — I want him back. I don't think I've ever been like this. Will I pull out of this? When?

October 5, 2003

A week. It's been a week since my Charlie died. A Sunday. A long, sad Sunday. Now Sunday is his day. I burn a big candle in a golden-colored glass. I've placed cut plumes of pampas grass around him. What else can I do? My mind only wants to think of him. Still so sad. One day there will be more happy thoughts, about all his cute and funny and endearing ways. There were hundreds, maybe thousands of these. But for now my mind is stuck in a terrifying sadness. I'm pushing myself to do things that make me happy. Like going to Montecito and visiting Botanik Nursery in Summerland. Like walking Barney and seeing his beautiful happy tail. Like maybe going to a movie tonight. Like anything that will make a dent in this. It's early morning, and Charlie's candle burns brightly. That helps. And Barney's barking. Lovely sound.

October 6, 2003

Slight bit better today.

Some good thoughts about Charlie: his persistence, his strength, his nonstoppableness. I loved how strong and determined he was — I would laugh when he would literally dig his heels in and not move another inch. I guess I encouraged his strong will, his stubbornness. And I would laugh so much when I saw him get fixated about something: not wanting to go for a walk, not wanting to change food, insisting on being petted in a certain spot, and more.

Oh, I know there will be more great dogs. After all, Barney is a great dog. But Charlie, he was almost human. So intuitive, my pal. I felt bigger, better, more confident just having him around, being in his presence.

A week and a day. A long week and a day. How is it possible that I won't see him again?

October 7, 2003

I know I am lucky to have had such a magnificent dog. Will I ever again have such a connection? I go for a walk, and I can feel him with me. I see him stopping, sniffing, getting aggressive. I see him smiling, wagging his tail.

Memories. I can retrieve memories. Looked through some old photo albums tonight and saw many pictures of my Charlie. Mostly when he was younger. What a character. Always looked busy. Saw pictures of when we first brought him home. Sturdy, blond little boy. He was adorable. In a flash the fourteen years went by.

Charlie, you were the best dog. Your loyalty. Your sense of humor. I will never forget your ways. Ways you figured out how to keep us connected. It's so hard not having, not feeling that connection. My big Golden. I miss you terribly. Rest in peace, my big guy.

October 9, 2003

Almost two weeks. We got four condolence cards. That felt good — some very special sentiments about Charlie.

Barney is helping me so much. He and I are home together tonight. We both just got back from Starbucks. I take him with me as much as possible. He loves socializing and being out and about, and I love having him with me. A Golden Retriever, yet so different from Charlie. Charlie just wanted to be in his house with his family. He had some interest in toys when he was young, but not much. Mostly he would like holding them in his mouth. No retrieving or ball playing. Life was a much more serious venture than that. Charlie was on the lookout. He was quite a bit more suspicious of people and much more interested in being protective than Barney. Cautious. A touch of something else besides Golden, perhaps.

I'm left with such wonderful memories of Charlie. I loved how he could be so serious and then in an instant do something goofy. Roll on his back with his feet in the air, back up into my lap and sit — all one hundred pounds of him for most of his life. Sometimes I'd be lying on the floor, and he'd come over and lie across me, actually pin me down, with that big smile on his face. I couldn't get up, mostly because I'd be laughing so hard. I'd have to call David to get him off of me. Charlie seemed so proud of that behavior.

Charlie, do you hear me? I miss all your wonderful antics. I miss your smiling face. I miss you looking for me. I miss you sitting in the middle of my paperwork on the floor. I miss each and every one of your ways. Oh how I miss you sitting with me while I sat on the floor putting on my makeup. Sliding down my back and sitting so we touched, back to back, and I know both of us could have sat there for hours.

And I miss how knowing you were. And your enthusiasm — it was so hard watching it wane the last few months. Although I saw it almost right to the end, until your physical body couldn't keep up with your so vibrant, energetic mind. Charlie, I'm so proud of how hard you tried at everything. And I know you stayed alive as long as you possibly could, and maybe a little longer. Thank you, dear Charlie, for giving me as much as you possibly could of yourself. Thank you for bonding with me. I just hope I gave you everything you wanted and made your life as happy and full as you made mine. Bless you, my big guy. I know I will miss you forever.

October 13, 2003

A holiday Monday, Columbus Day. The weather has turned hot and clear, the sky blue, a welcome relief from the month or more of fog. A good day, mostly because I kept busy. One patient, then it was off to Calvin's Nursery, then some shopping, then home briefly, and finally to a movie — *School of Rock*. A happy movie. So no time to be sad. Charlie is in my mind constantly, but these were wonderful distractions.

Charlie, thank you for being such a great dog. You were so loyal and protective, and yet sweet and gentle at the same time. I miss you so very much. Your strength, your handsome face, the big grin you would get when you saw me, and so much more. The house feels strange and empty without you.

And Barney, he misses you too. I can tell. He looks so lost at times, doesn't act perky the way he did when you were here. He misses his dad, his alpha dog. He looked up to you so much. Remember how he deferred to you, how he would check in with you, kiss your nose, stand so you could smell him, watch you for cues? He was a perfect pack member, wasn't he, Charlie? And you were good to him too. You would let him take toys out of your mouth — you knew he was such a baby. You were such a good dad.

We have to continue on without you, Charlie, but you left us with so, so much. Know that we all love you and thank you for all you gave. I hope we gave you enough.

October 16, 2003

Sad, sad days. Can't pull myself out of it. I struggle through, but it seems like it's getting worse. I miss my big guy so much. I can't imagine ever loving another dog like that. And I can't imagine another dog loving me the way Charlie did. I ache. Please someone make this pain go away. What would help? Maybe just time. I do get a little lost in my gardening and still find some relief in that.

Charlie, you made me happier than any being I have ever known. Thank you for giving me such joy. I know you knew you made me happy. You would purposely do things, like kissing on the lips when I would come home, like giving me that side glance, like lying across me on the floor and pinning me down. Or coming to find me in the house or garden. I miss all of that, and more. I can't say it enough how much I miss you. Time. More time. We're only coming on three weeks.

October 18, 2003

Beautiful day. Clear blue sky, warm, but not too hot. And a trip up the coast to Montecito and Summerland: David, Barney, and me. A change of scenery. Helped so much. Some of my favorite haunts — Botanik, Pane e Vino, Pierre La Fond — and the whole atmosphere, especially in Montecito. Barney was his usual ever-so-friendly self. How will he ever be alpha dog?

I felt better being outside, moving around. This morning, some gardening, mostly watering. Later, encountering friendly people. For example, at Pane e Vino, the waiter, who knew Barney was in our car, brought him some water — with three ice cubes! Outside the restaurant, there was a two-year-old black Brussels Griffon, Cassie. Barney played with her a little, made him so happy. I loved seeing that. At Botanik, they threw in a thyme plant for free. The salesman said it looked as if it needed love.

It was just one of those days where everything seemed to work. I even rescued a monarch butterfly from a spider web, got it out safely and without hurting it. Beautiful orange wings. After I pulled it out, it flew onto a tree limb, and then proceeded to follow me while I watered, at one point flying right near my face!

A lighter day, some joy in my heart. I guess it's a process, with ups and downs. Charlie, it was a little easier today. Rest in peace, you big, gentle old soul.

October 22, 2003

Took Barney to Leo Carrillo State Park and Beach. He liked the park but went crazy at the beach. He was ecstatic. Started jumping, prancing. Ran in and out of the water. I loved seeing him so happy. Right now he's sound asleep on the bed. He has his paw wrapped around goofy dog, one of his little stuffed toys. Good night, happy Barney.

October 24, 2003

A Friday. It's a bit better. Don't know if it's temporary, but the ache is subsiding. I think I'm a little numb. Part of me knows I can't go on functioning with a gaping wound, that I must find a way to heal it. So I've tried to keep busy. I spent just about all my free time this week gardening and, mostly, being with Barney. As a matter of fact, as I'm writing this, he's throwing his paw at me and demanding to be petted. He has his face in my lap and is staring up at me, lying on his side on the bed. He wants love and attention, and I'm more than happy to give it to him. I know that he, too, misses Charlie. The whole house misses Charlie.

It's so different now. Charlie's energy and spirit were so big, grand, noble, joyful, solid, and strong. I miss his gorgeous face, which lit up when he was happy. Is this all going to fade, and am I going to be left with only a few wisps of memories? I must just keep persevering through. A few weeks ago, the pain was excruciating. Now, it's been four weeks, and it's a little easier. Maybe that's because I have distracted myself so much this week, but maybe it's going to hit me like a ton of bricks again.

Charlie, you were the best dog, buddy, sidekick, confidant a person could have. You did your job perfectly. I felt so protected when you were around. And your loyalty was unswerving. I love how your family meant everything to you and I love how I was the center of your world. You were the center of mine. And so now I'm a little lost, a little off, and I have to get situated again.

Please know I love you and always will, with all my heart and soul. Rest, my little boy, my puppy, my pal.

October 25, 2003

A little easier again today, Puppy. We went to Montecito. Barney, David and I. And I remembered how much fun you had at San Ysidro Ranch in June. Do you remember that? You loved it up there. Remember Rose Cottage? You were so eager and happy, and you adapted in a day. You loved your walks. You slept on your big round bed. Your appetite was tremendous. We have lots of pictures of you. You were so alert. For five whole days. I am so glad we took you up there. And you let Barney be a bit of a leader. That was good of you. Can't believe that was only in June. It's October, and I don't get to see and feel that gorgeous face and that very powerful energy. I love thinking about you at San Ysidro Ranch, thinking about you being happy. Mostly I love just thinking about you. Good night, my Puppy. Today was a better day.

October 26, 2003

A month. A month. Seems longer. Seems shorter. No real sense of time. Sad. It's a Sunday. I think about Charlie lots on Sundays. Born of the sun. Dies on a Sunday. So sad. He's gone. My little pillar. My joy. My little-guy-big-guy, who made me laugh. Been holding back the tears all day.

The time changed today. Fall back. An extra hour. Haven't changed one clock. Don't care.

I miss you so much, Charlie. Hard to believe you're gone. Maybe I wasn't busy enough today. Santa Ana winds. Hot, lots of watering. All day. Will I ever not miss you, Charlie? I just want to live in the happy memories of you. Will that ever be possible? My grand dog. Only one Charlie. I'm lucky, but I want more Charlie. Fourteen years, not enough. Well, I've run out of words. I love you, Charlie. Goodnight, my boy.

November 2, 2003

Sunday. Spent a few hours at work today. One patient. Thought about Charlie a lot. I think about him every day, but some days more than others. I thought about a day, a long time ago, when he was about three years old …

I am out in the garden, and from a distance I can see him walking over to me with something pretty big in his mouth. A little prance to his step. He gets closer. I see it's a big round rock. He looks pleased with himself. I ask him to give it to me, telling him it's not good for his teeth to be carrying that, smiling all the while as I'm talking to him. He drops it in my hand. I tell him what a good boy he is, that it's a great present. He looks even more pleased with himself. He walks off back into the garden among the trees and the African daisies …

It's eleven years later, and I still have that rock, at my office. I use it to stabilize a large green-and-beige-striped basket that holds dark green eucalyptus branches. Whenever I look at that basket, I think of that day and how happy Charlie was with himself, the smile he had on his face. How good he was, and how solid. It's a wonderful memory. That day, that rock, and Charlie.

Charlie in the African daisies

Twenty-Two

November 9, 2003

Surprises. Went to a continuing-education seminar on animal-assisted therapy today — you never know where some healing will come from. I knew I'd hear about and see pictures of Goldens, because of their temperament and ability to connect. But I never anticipated that the instructor's love of his life, his dog who lived for fourteen years and died three years ago and was of course a Golden, was named "Puppy." That was her real name. The instructor had rescued her from the streets — teeth and everything else a mess — and cleaned her up, loved her, and worked with her like a colleague, for most of her life as a therapy dog. He was so in love with her.

The instructor works not only with dogs but also with birds. Also has fish and a lizard. His passion for what he does comes pouring out of him in story after story of how he helps people open up and how they become healed through connecting with animals. So primal. And guess what — he said he became interested in and fell in love with animals after seeing the movie *Charly*.

But when he started talking about "Puppy," his soul attachment, who probably helped him more than any other being, I lost it.

Tears, but it was a good cry. I knew exactly what he meant. And her name was Puppy like Charlie, and she was a Golden like Charlie, and she lived fourteen years like Charlie.

How does something like this happen, at such a right time? It was so touching, so cathartic, so amazing, and it helped me so much. Hearing his story, hearing the name Puppy throughout the day, hearing and seeing his love for her. And seeing all the pictures of Goldens.

He spoke of the importance of our connection with animals, but he never really got into analyzing it. I don't think we yet have the words, may never have.

Then at the end of the day, he spoke of one of his patients, a child, who had not been in to see him for several months, during which time Puppy had died. When the child came and of course asked for Puppy, the instructor had to tell him what happened. The boy, seven years old, wanted to know if he would ever see her again. At first, the instructor did not know how to answer, but after a moment he said that Puppy was a blessing. The little boy then asked, "What is a blessing?" To which the instructor replied, "A blessing is something that makes us a more complete human being."

November 13, 2003

I had a dream about Charlie last night. He was around six years old. His coat was full and thick, and he was filled with energy. He was playing with a Golden Retriever puppy. A blonde little girl, who adored him. She was chasing him, nipping at him, wouldn't leave him alone. Charlie was so patient with her, watched her intently, smiling the whole time.

Yesterday, there was a light rain. Today, a clear sky, crisp air. Invigorating. Mostly I was in the garden. Fertilizing, raking, watering, potting. Even cleaned my shovels and clippers. Later I took Barney to play ball, in a big, open field. He was so happy chasing that ball, running back and forth with it excitedly.

It was a beautiful day. A day that sparkled from beginning to end. In my dream, I loved seeing Charlie with that little girl, having so much fun. I remembered how happy he was in his home, in his garden, with his family. Today, so was I.

CHARLIE

November 14, 2003

End of the week. Friday. Lots of errands. One bringing dog food, dog biscuits, baby food, and more to the animal shelter, on behalf of Charlie. That felt good. Saw a woman there with a kitten that had been abandoned. Just a few days old, tiniest thing. The stories people must hear working there.

So after David and I dropped off these bags of dog goodies, we took some biscuits to all the dogs in the kennels. Liva-Snaps — same as the ones we gave to Charlie at the end, when we were giving him anything he would eat. Most of the dogs in the shelter got really happy with the biscuits, though a few were too scared or upset to take them.

It felt good to give to the shelter what we had gotten for Charlie. When I handed the animal control officer the two bags, I told her they were from Charlie, our fourteen-year-old Golden, whom we just lost.

"Fourteen years, that's a nice long life," she said.

Yes, indeed, I thought.

Epilogue

December 30, 2008

San Ysidro Ranch. David and I have come up for a brief stay. I just went on an early morning walk, lush vegetation everywhere. They say the place is full, yet it's still so quiet. I think people come here looking for that.

Walked by Rose Cottage. Lots of thoughts about you, Charlie. How happy you were here. Your eagerness on your walks. How much you loved meeting everyone. Your tail gently wagging, that smile. My big Golden.

Our cottage this time has a great view of the ocean over the trees, decks all around, private. I could stay here for a very long time. Though we must leave today.

But for a moment, I've had a chance to be close to you, my Charlie, in a place that you loved. Now your spirit lives here, too. My beautiful boy. My buddy. I love you, sweet Charlie. Always will.

We'll do this again, soon.

Charlie and me

Acknowledgments

Telling Charlie's story was a labor of love. And I have many people to thank for their contributions.

From the start, my husband David believed in this story and my ability to tell it. With his poet's eye and ear and mastery of the English language, as well as with his understanding of Charlie and me, David edited my manuscript meticulously and very thoughtfully, too many times to mention. His insights contributed tremendously. Most importantly, David always supported my very deep and special relationship with Charlie. I am so thankful for all that David gave to this story, to Charlie, and to me.

Susan Pagani, a highly skilled editor at Langdon Street Press who just happens to love dogs and — even though she lives in Minnesota — also loves gardens, understood Charlie's story at its core and on many of the levels I had intended. I'm so grateful to Susan for her gentle guidance and her extraordinary attention to detail. Unfortunately, Susan changed careers before the editing of my manuscript was completed, so I had to find another editor.

That search led me to Cliff Carle, an author who seems to live and breathe books, from editing to publishing to marketing. Cliff comprehensively edited my manuscript, providing me with helpful reasoning for almost every recommendation. And I so appreciated Cliff's no-nonsense, bottom-line approach and timely responses, as well as his sense of humor. He contributed a great deal.

My very intelligent friend, artist, and cousin Myrna Orenbach Dwyer so carefully edited Charlie's story a number of times. Besides being an excellent grammarian, she too loves animals and gardens. I'm so thankful to Myrna not only for her perceptive help with my manuscript but also for her encouragement and support of me and this story. And I'm so happy she's my cousin.

By the time my manuscript got to Ron Kenner, a longtime editor, for the "final" edit, I thought there would be nothing to find except some typographical errors. Although Ron did find a few of those, more importantly he suggested some substantive edits that I know made this story even better. Ron was easy to work with and very responsive. I so appreciated his involvement.

After my manuscript had been edited to my satisfaction, I asked two editors — Pam Guerrieri and Cris Devine — to proofread it. They found very few changes, which reassured me that my manuscript was ready to go to my publisher. Both had a genuine feel for Charlie's story and were touched by it. I thank Pam and Cris greatly.

Additionally, Pam was quite knowledgeable not only about current trends in grammar but also about Langdon Street and its publishing process. She willingly and enthusiastically helped me make some final grammatical choices as well as other decisions. I liked her aesthetic sensibilities, and she was very generous both with her time and her knowledge. Thank you so much, Pam.

Tom Puckett, Ron Kenner's assistant, gave my manuscript the actual final proofread, with strict instructions to leave all commas alone — by that point I was dreaming about them! Fortunately, Tom found just about nothing. Voilà! My manuscript was ready to go. Thank you, Tom.

Early on in the process, Dorothy Wall, an author and editor, gave me some sage advice about my manuscript and about publishing, and I appreciated her ideas.

Many thanks to the staff at Langdon Street Press for their assistance in getting Charlie's story onto the printed page. All were very patient, thoughtful, and quick to respond throughout this process.

Many thanks also to Roger Wong at Samy's Camera, who so painstakingly and patiently worked with my pictures and graphics, from enhancing to sizing to adding borders, and who provided invaluable assistance in creating the final versions of my front and back covers.

Dennis Palumbo, an author, writing coach, and psychotherapist, listened to my journal entries as this book was being born and enthusiastically encouraged me to keep on writing. Dennis is a great motivator.

I want to thank my dedicated, reliable, and compassionate gardener, Jesus Castro, for all he gave to my garden, for the joy of working with him, and for the peace of mind I was able to have in knowing he was tending my garden while I was caring for Charlie. Jesus made my garden and my life so much better.

Rick Sacks at Turk Hessellund Nursery in Montecito, California, carefully reviewed my manuscript to ensure that its gardening information was correct. He has also been responsible for imbuing me with much of the horticultural knowledge I've gained over the years. I always look forward to my trips to Turk's because I know he's there.

And horticulturalist John Greenlee, one of the foremost authorities on grasses in the United States, took time out of his busy day to provide me with so much information about bamboos, particularly the otatea variety. I think I now know most of what there is to know about otatea, my favorite bamboo.

To Dr. Robert Olds, who so graciously agreed to write the foreword to Charlie's story, who read my manuscript several times, and who so caringly and with extraordinary skill took care of my Charlie for Charlie's whole life: I want to thank you from the bottom of my heart.

I want to thank Dr. Karen Martin for her wisdom and knowledge in caring for Charlie, both of which helped Charlie so much. Dr. Lisa Newell was there for Charlie at some very key moments. Her support was invaluable. Dr. Beth Brockman took Charlie under her medical wing at a critical time in Charlie's life and attended to him diligently until he was much better. I am so grateful to each of you.

And to my uncle Max Orenbach, who loved nature, always believed in me, and encouraged me to reach for the stars, I thank you, again.

CHARLIE

It might go without saying, but I want to thank my beautiful Charlie, who of course made this book possible. No one could have been a more loyal and loving companion. My inspiration. The most indomitable spirit I have ever known. My once-in-a-lifetime dog.

About the Author

Barbara Lampert is a Marriage and Family Therapist. She specializes in relationships and has a doctorate in medical sociology and two master's degrees. Charlie was a puppy when she was studying for her therapist's license.

Barbara has a private psychotherapy practice in Brentwood, California, where she sees individuals, couples, and families. Sometimes her patients bring their dogs to their sessions, which is just fine with her.

All Barbara's life, she's loved dogs. She's been told that from the time she could walk, she would run up to any dog she saw, no matter the size. As a child, she yearned for a dog but was never given one. So after she became an adult, she filled her life with dogs: a Cairn Terrier mix, an Afghan Hound, a Sheltie, but mostly Golden Retrievers. She loves how wonderfully Goldens connect — with people, with other breeds, with each other.

Barbara lives in Malibu, California, with her husband David and their six-year-old Golden Retriever, Harry.

She has no children. All she's ever wanted are dogs.

You can learn more about *Charlie: A Love Story* by visiting www.charliealovestory.com.